RANDOM RECOLLECTIONS OF A PERIPATETIC PHYSICIST

Jasper McKee

MINERVA PRESS
LONDON
ATLANTA MONTREUX SYDNEY

RANDOM RECOLLECTIONS OF A PERIPATETIC
PHYSICIST
Copyright © Jasper McKee 1998

All Rights Reserved

No part of this book may be reproduced in any form,
by photocopying or by any electronic or mechanical means,
including information storage or retrieval systems,
without permission in writing from both the copyright
owner and the publisher of this book.

ISBN 0 75410 300 5

First Published 1998 by
MINERVA PRESS
195 Knightsbridge
London SW7 1RE

Printed in Great Britain for Minerva Press

RANDOM RECOLLECTIONS OF A PERIPATETIC PHYSICIST

To Conor and Siobhan; in memory of Christine.

Acknowledgement

The author thanks Wanda Klassen for her tireless enthusiasm and faultless accuracy in deciphering and interpreting the original manuscript.

Foreword

This book is not an autobiography. It is, rather, a collection of vignettes, cautionary tales and humorous anecdotes reflecting the interaction between a physicist and the social environment in which he finds himself. The chapters cover a period of about fifty years, first drawing a portrait of the physicist as a young man and then following him through four countries and two continents to his present haven as Professor Emeritus in the Department of Physics at the University of Manitoba in Winnipeg, Canada.

The impetus for writing this book came from the public perception that physicists are collectively incomprehensible, disquieting and perhaps irrelevant to those in the real world. For this reason, the book contains little fundamental physics and paints no detailed portraits of physicists, eminent or otherwise. It does however attempt to illuminate the various environments in which scientists work, educate, bring up their families and communicate their specialism. Indeed the arena within which the academic physicist works will hopefully be seen as one in which occasional humour if not persistent hilarity plays a prominent role. For those readers interested in hard science, the two hundred or so scientific papers and chapters of books already published by the author are readily available through library and computer. This book however is not concerned with such weighty matters. It merely deals with everyday life, the part that a physicist plays in it, and the fact that he or she is often transformed by it.

Contents

One	The Family of the Physicist	11
Two	Becoming a Physicist	18
Three	The Physicist as a Graduate Student	32
Four	The Physicist Discovers Local Politics	44
Five	The Physicist as a Journalist and Observer of Our Times	51
Six	The Physicist at Play	66
Seven	The Physicist as a Thespian	73
Eight	The Physicist at Birmingham University	76
Nine	The Physicist Meets Experimental Equipment and Researchers at Birmingham	92
Ten	The Physicist Goes Courting and Plans a Honeymoon	104
Eleven	The Physicist Visits Oxford in Winter	123
Twelve	The Physicist at the University of California, Berkeley	127

Thirteen	The Physicist as a Babysitter	132
Fourteen	The Physicist Goes to the University of Manitoba	136
Fifteen	The Physicist Recalls Anecdotal Tales of the Cavendish Laboratory as Told in Cambridge in 1982	147
Sixteen	The Physicist as a Musician	155
Seventeen	The Physicist has Problems with Air, Fire and Water	163
Eighteen	The Physicist Aspires to Political Office	171
Nineteen	The Physicist as a Scientific Communicator	180
Twenty	Physics in Everyday Life	193

Chapter One

The Family of the Physicist

On the 6th June, 1930, I was born a son to Captain James and Mrs Dorothy McKee, of 35 Cyprus Park, Bloomfield, Belfast. I was christened James Stanley Colton, later to be known as Jasper, and was to become the physicist whose observations form the bulk of this book.[1]

The McKees had, for many years, been in the linen business. Both my dad and his brother, William Dickson McKee, were noted sportsmen in the North of Ireland in their early years, playing first-class football and cricket for the amateur team Cliftonville. Both enlisted for duty in the First World War with unfortunate results. Willie was killed in 1916 at the Battle of the Somme and my father-to-be lost a leg at the Battle of Messines Ridge, having been promoted to the rank of major on the battlefield. Jim was invalided out of the forces, recovered in England, and later went on to marry my mother, Dorothy Colton, in 1925.

There were three other members of the McKee family, Jim's sisters, Nanny, Janet and Anna, who proved tremendously supportive to their nephew in later years.

---

[1] Shortly after his birth, the family decided to leave Belfast for the more romantic environment of County Down. They only just made it; 33 Stormont Park being exactly one house outside the city boundary.

The Great War of 1914–1918 decimated many families in the North of Ireland. Most regiments in the expeditionary forces were drawn from local communities and very often all the men from whole families and towns would be virtually wiped out in a single battle. Toddling and growing up in the Thirties and the Forties made a child particularly aware of the absence of menfolk. Most of my father's male cousins and more remote relatives had also disappeared from the scene long before I was to join it.

My mother, Dorothy Colton, had a father of Cornish descent who was born in Ballygally Castle on the Antrim Coast Road. He would later change his name from John Colton to John Macauley Colton because he thought it sounded more interesting and businesslike. He became Managing Director of Robert Watson & Company, the foremost furniture store in Belfast in the late 1930s. His wife, my grandmother, was born Sophie Elizabeth Workman and came from a close knit family in Coleraine. Dorothy, my mother, had two sisters: my aunt Norah and another sister, Eileen, who had died when she was twenty-one.

My parents' first child, Beatrice Elizabeth, was born in 1929 and died several weeks after birth, so when I came along in 1930, I became the eldest son of James and Dorothy McKee. The arrival of my brother, on the 30th October, 1933, was a more than welcome addition to the family but, unfortunately, it was a mere nine months after that event when my father died from complications following an operation for appendicitis and gallstones.

I, personally, can only clearly remember my father from one occasion. He was, at the time, the headmaster's private secretary at Campbell College, the school that I would eventually attend. He would come home to our house on Stormont Park through a little red gate set in the wall around the college, and then walk approximately thirty yards to where we lived. Having lost the leg and having a prosthesis, of sorts, in place, he preferred to wear plus-fours which were popular in the Thirties and, indeed, suited him well from later photographs that I have seen. I remember on one occasion seeing him come through the little red gate and my running, as only a little lad can do, to grab him around the legs somewhere below the knees in a welcome of childish simplicity. I believe that he was a warm, kind-hearted and perceptive father but I never really knew him.

The advent of my young brother, Ian, was not welcomed by his brother with the type of enthusiasm that one might normally expect. After his birth, I was noted to be morose and withdrawn a considerable amount of the time until one famous morning when I was found to be leaping up and down and chuckling with delight, saying, 'It's funny, it's funny!' My mother thought this was, under the circumstances, an alarming incident and went to look for Ian, only to find his pram covered from top to bottom with additional blankets that I apparently thought would solve whatever problem I imagined existed. This apocryphal tale, for whose veracity I cannot really account, has fortunately long been forgotten and my brother has flourished despite my efforts to somewhat curtail his well-being at the age of one.

The rest of the 1930s remain for the most part a blur in memory. I do remember being on holiday in Cloghey with my grandparents and mother in 1937, when people were fearfully discussing news of the Spanish Civil War. In the same year, I went to Cabin Hill, Campbell College Preparatory School, which was situated in the Knock area of Belfast. Because of the position my father had held at Campbell College on his death, I was allowed entry to the school some three years earlier than normal entry level and paid fees equivalent to those for sons of clergymen, which apparently was a major reduction. Being fairly bright and intelligent, but generally impossible, I was subjected to a considerable amount of bullying and personal belabourment and, in the early years at school, life was far from a bed of roses.

At the age of seven also, my eyesight deteriorated from being perfect to being almost non-existent due to a muscular condition of the eye, and for two years I was not allowed to read anything myself. My mother read texts and it was up to me to learn the contents and to dictate the answers to questions. This exercise seemed to stimulate my brain for I succeeded in winning an entrance scholarship at the age of eleven which set me on a track that was to be pretty profitable in the future. From the age of eleven to the completion of my graduate work at university, I depended only on such scholarships as were available at preparatory school, senior school, university, and graduate school.

It was at the age of nine, while attending the headmaster's Latin class, that I was entrusted with the name Jasper which replaced the three options, James, Stanley and Colton, given to me by my parents at birth. Mr S.W.V. Sutton, the headmaster, was an able academic and always seemed to require additional academic challenges. He decided to give all twenty or so members of his senior Latin class a name that was not their own, was biblical in character, and started with the letter 'J'. Names such as Jezreel, Jeroboam, Jehoiakim, Joshua, and so forth were spread around the class. The name I received seemed to come from the bottom of his barrel of names, appearing only in the Book of Revelation, where it is written 'the foundations thereof were of jasper'. Jasper as a given name seemed only tenuously related to those of biblical luminaries presented to the rest of the class. In the month previous to my acquisition of the name Jasper, my colleague at the next desk, whose real name was Howard Brown, rejoiced in the name Jasper. I have no recollection of the name to which I responded during that time, but once the name Jasper was donated to me, it was merely a year before I was forced, for reasons of usage, to sign my Christmas cards Jasper McKee.

When war broke out in the autumn of 1939, my maternal grandfather, John M. Colton, had recently died. Nightly blackouts of cities and towns were initiated, gas masks were issued to all members of the population, bomb shelters were created, and many nights and weekends were spent putting masking tape over windows to minimise injury from the shattering of glass. Bombing of the city of Belfast, when it began in the early months of 1941, proved to be regular and devastating. The Republic of Ireland being neutral in the war provided visible landmarks for fleets of bombers making their way up the coast of Ireland to the shipyards and industrial heartland of Northern Ireland. Night after night, my mother and I and my young brother would sit under a breakfast table that had been moved beneath the stairs hoping that this flimsy structure would provide useful protection from the chaos around us. As an eleven year old I can remember very well the fiery scene around us at night once the all-clear had sounded and the visiting aeroplanes had done their worst.

Around Easter time, my mother decided that enough was enough and we evacuated ourselves to Portrush on the North Antrim Coast. Campbell College had already left its premises in Belfast which were to serve as a military hospital and moved to the Northern Counties hotel in Portrush. For the two years of our exile on the north coast of Ireland, I was permitted to go to Campbell College, despite the fact that I was several years younger than any of the other students studying there. I was a day boy, whereas most of the others were boarders. However, the opportunity to attend school, to play sports on five afternoons of the week, and to be free from air raids and air raid sirens was a comparative delight after the difficulties of the previous six months. Experiencing the wild Atlantic Ocean in the winter was also a stimulating experience, and the freedom to walk along the coast road to Dunluce Castle and the Giant's Causeway stood in sharp contrast to the claustrophobic confines of a city at war. Only the regular missions of the Portrush lifeboat to rescue survivors from torpedoed ships reminded us of the realities of the political situation.

When the Battle of Britain was over and victory in Europe appeared to be imminent, the McKee family returned to 33 Stormont Park where our home still stood intact.

After a couple of years of further study at Cabin Hill, which had become a senior school in our absence, Campbell College returned to its old location and, for my final four years of school, the campus at Belmont was to be a peaceful haven for intellectual growth and healthy activity.

In the post-war era, much of life returned to normal and new and different opportunities for travel and personal advancement appeared on the horizon. Mother stayed in Belfast where she died in 1988. Both my brother, Ian, and I eventually moved abroad to greener pastures and new challenges. Ian, after completing his diploma in architecture from the School of Art in Edinburgh, obtained his ARIBA (Associate of the Royal Institute of British Architects) and then specialised in town planning. He joined the United Nations Development Program and, for forty years until his retirement in 1995, worked in a variety of countries from Montserrat through Fiji to Bangladesh, Bhutan, and even Burma. While in Kenya he met and married his wife, Janet, and they have three sons, James, Andrew and David.

I, myself, after a frenetic period of bachelordom, finally fell hopelessly in love with a young first-year social science student, Christine Savage, while a lecturer at Birmingham

University. We were married in 1961 and have two children, Conor, a logistics officer in the Canadian Navy, and Siobhan, a veterinarian and small animal dermatologist, currently practising in the south of England. Both are married and spend much of their time attempting to keep the physicist under control. Christine sadly, after a marvellous career as Social Policy Consultant, University Ombudsman, City Councillor, and finally Professor of City Planning in the Faculty of Architecture of the University of Manitoba, succumbed to breast cancer in the summer of 1995. She was an inspiration to us all.

Chapter Two

Becoming a Physicist

It was always inevitable that I would go to university despite the fact that no member of my family had previously darkened the hallowed halls. My scientific career evolved painlessly, if not effortlessly, at the hands of teachers, advisers, family members, and peers of all kinds. Campbell College, the school that I attended, was academically oriented while also taking a more than healthy interest in athletic pursuits. By the time I had reached the age of sixteen, I had unconsciously specialised in a variety of scientific subjects with only French, History and English adding enrichment and breadth to my programme. Giving up Latin at the age of fifteen had left me with little formal classical education in view.

While passing the lower sixth level of education (roughly equivalent to Grade 11 in Canada), a new headmaster came to the college, fresh with enthusiasm for chemistry and with a youthful and dynamic teaching style. Immediately, chemistry became my discipline of choice, and in the long vacation before sixth form I devoted most of my time to building a thermostatically controlled tank with which to carry out chemical reaction experiments in my final year (Grade 12, as it would be considered in Canada).

The budding chemist however suffered another conversion on the road to graduation from high school. A new teacher with a PhD arrived to teach physics in the sixth form. He was not only excited about the thirty-seven aurorae that he had photographed and studied as part of his degree, but was full of the excitement of quantum mechanics, the discovery of new particles, and a gamut of esoteric phenomena previously unheard of by the students that he was teaching. Dr George Humphries unleashed the physicist in Jasper McKee and he himself went on to become headmaster of Coleraine Academical Institution and to instil the excitement of academic study in a wide variety of eager and willing students.

I progressed to the Queen's University of Belfast in the autumn of 1948. At that time there were two important prerequisites to acceptance by the university. Firstly, one was required to matriculate. This entailed either the accumulation of a number of Oxford and Cambridge School Certificate results or adequate performance in several subjects at A level in the higher certification examinations. Alternatively, performance in the local Northern Ireland Senior Certificate examinations could qualify a student for entry to university. The second factor determining entry to the university lay in the ability to pay fees, costs of accommodation, and food and travel expenses, in much the same way as these are important today.

Prior to completion of the sixth form curriculum, I was informed by the Education Committee of County Down, where I resided, that I had been awarded one of the top scholarships to Queen's University, Belfast, and that I was to be congratulated on this feat. This being the case, I determined I would go there, live at home, and use the scholarship for payment of fees and incidental support costs.

Because of the variety of means of matriculation, students took a mixture of courses in their first year of study, depending on their educational background. The undergraduate science syllabus was of four years' duration but what you studied in first year tended to greatly influence the details of your degree in later years. One subject of particular importance to an embryonic physicist is mathematics and on my first day of classes I turned up for the first-year mathematics lecture only to find that the lecture theatre was so full and overflowing that even seats on the stairs were difficult to come by. The class of two hundred or so was in sharp contrast to the classes of twenty-five that I had attended at Campbell College. The students in this class were informed, however, that if they had performed creditably in the A level examination and felt confident enough to proceed, they might, instead of taking first-year mathematics, take the second-year mathematics class. At the end of the year, if a student did not do well enough to pass this more advanced course, he or she might still be awarded the first-year mathematics completion certificate. This would then enable the student to proceed to a second year of university study without delay. I immediately decided to attend the second-year mathematics class only to find that it also contained well in excess of one hundred people and access to the instructor would again be difficult. However, it so happened that the lecturer for this course was happy to announce that people who felt that they might have little difficulty with the second-year ordinary mathematics course should consider attending the second-year honours mathematics class with the additional possibility that a less than satisfactory performance in the honours section might still merit a pass in the second-year ordinary mathematics class. A considerably inferior performance might still be taken as equivalent to satisfactory performance in the first-year mathematics class. So I turned up for the first lecture in second-year honours mathematics to find, to my delight, that the entire number of people involved was around thirty, that the head of the department was personally teaching the course, and that the mathematics itself was totally different to any that I had followed before. Proving that a continuous function of a continuous function is itself continuous was much more exciting to my mind than solving first order differential equations in a cast of thousands. At the end of the year, it transpired that all members of the second-year honours class performed satisfactorily and that all students could move directly into the degree syllabus in mathematics. This course could be completed in one further year of study. So, in my second year at Queen's University, I completed the requirements for a pass degree in mathematics without specifically graduating in that discipline. This fortuitous event coloured my decision to become a theoretical physicist on completion of my undergraduate physics degree.

One of the final entry years at which the vice-chancellor of the university personally shook hands with all matriculating students was 1948. I was one of the last students to formally matriculate and can still remember the red and swollen hand that was offered to me by Sir David Lindsay-Keir on this welcoming, if archaic, occasion. So, I was now a university student and ready for action.

I have always regarded myself as fortunate in being exposed to first-year instructors of the calibre of Dr Cecil Wilson, in chemistry, and Professor Karl Emeleus, in physics, the latter being the head of the physics department. Early impressions and learning habits are of immense importance to the student.

The first meeting between lecturer and class was, however, a revelation to me. Exactly on the hour, a very impressive military figure strode into the lecture room and outlined in stentorian tones the schedule of laboratory classes and the times and venues of succeeding lectures. We were all highly impressed with the demeanour, appearance and vocabulary of this person as he laid out, in no uncertain terms, our course of study. It came therefore as a great surprise to all of us to discover later that this was in fact the laboratory technician and not the great man himself. On completion of his introductory remarks, the elegant assistant left confidently by one door while a small, frail-looking waif of a man slipped in through another door and stood before us in a brown jacket with at least one of the elbows missing.

Professor Emeleus, indeed, looked more like the gardener than the head of the department as he first appeared before us. But lecture content is always more important than personal appearance, and physics as a discipline came alive through his logic and language.

The transition from school to university was not, however, without its unwelcome vicissitudes. Some three weeks after the commencement of term, there was no sign of funds from County Down Education Authority being deposited either in my bank account or at the university. I, therefore, determined to visit the Education Department offices and made an appointment with the secretary, whose name was Ferguson. I went for the interview in confidence and armed with the notification of scholarship award which I had received several months previously. What happened then, however, was beyond belief. Ferguson rose to his feet, walked up and down, and gave me a long dissertation to the effect that it was only appropriate that the County would have an award scheme similar to that of the City of Belfast and that eventually the scholarships awarded would be at the same level as those in the City of Belfast. Unfortunately, he was sorry to have to point out, the harvest for that particular year had been particularly bad and that the anticipated income to the County was significantly less than might normally have been anticipated. In particular, for that year only, all scholarships would be set at a level of no pounds, no shillings, and no pence, and whereas the scrolls themselves indicated the intention of the County, there would in fact be no financial award made to the happy recipients of any of the scholarships. At this point, I remember leaping to my feet, throwing my scholarship announcement on his desk, telling him in no uncertain terms that he had encouraged me to enrol at university under false pretences, and that his actions and the actions of the Education Committee, if not illegal, were certainly immoral. I resolved at that moment to ensure that, by the time I had finished my university career, scholarships from all areas of the province would be at the same level and be guaranteed to recipients. It was not, in fact, until I was a graduate student that I was instrumental in arranging for the Minister of Education for Northern Ireland, Mr Harry Midgley, to agree to the implementation of standardised awards across the province.

While digesting the import of my interview with Mr Ferguson, it was fortunately brought to my attention that I should be eligible for a Kitchener Scholarship which would be awarded from a fund set up to support university entrants who were the sons or daughters of veterans from either of the two world wars. It was a great relief, a surprise, and a proud moment for me when I obtained the financial security hoped for in my undergraduate studies through a synergy between my academic performance to that date and my father's gallant war record.

An interesting feature of first-year lectures at university was the roll call of students taken at the start of each lecture, and full-time attendance was expected of all the students. In order to facilitate this record keeping, all seats in the lecture theatre had large white numbers painted on the back of the seat. The assistant or technician who would record absences merely had to note the numbers that were visible from the podium in order to obtain a perfect record. The whole system, of course, depended upon people always sitting in the same seat and student names being recorded on a master chart at the start of the academic year.

In chemistry classes there was a student called West who kept on misjudging his seat and sitting in someone else's and creating such overall chaos that the lecturer each day would note the position of West before starting his lecture. West was always present but almost invariably marked absent and was not going to be allowed to sit the examination. The need to move West to his correct location became a dominant feature of all chemistry lectures from that time on. Witticisms in relation to the location of the student became frequent and phrases such as 'Gone West' or 'Sinking in the West' were used by the lecturer to identify the position taken in a given class. It is perhaps largely due to the efforts of West that the taking of attendance in lectures was finally terminated two years later.

At Queen's University, all the classes started and terminated according to university time. That is to say, a lecture would start five minutes past the hour giving time for students to arrive and take their places and would terminate five minutes before the hour so that students could go from one location to another. The hour was determined by the university clock which was set in one of the walls of the main quadrangle and chimed six times to denote each hour of the day. I once asked the bursar, George Burland, why that would be. He responded, very sensibly, that it took at least four or five chimes in order to draw the hour to the attention of the student. On the other hand, the lectures with the largest attendance took place at nine, ten, eleven and twelve o'clock in the morning. For the clock to chime nine, ten, eleven, or twelve times took an inordinate period of time and, as students tended to move fastest towards their classes on completion of the chimes, it was felt a compromise of six chimes per hour would both draw attention to the hour and activate students in a way that no other combination of reality and chimes could.

The physics lecture theatres and laboratories had a marvellously solid, permanent, and Victorian feeling to them. There was much stone and a great deal of polished wood in the areas where students were taught. Personification of pieces of equipment was common. Big Bertha was the large induction coil, and the Helmholtz Wagon was a set of conducting coils on a table made up to look for all the world like a covered wagon ready to head to the west. There was much elegant glassware in the laboratories, mercury vapour pumps, and combustion tubes that not only looked attractive but made possible the generation of a variety of gas discharges with their appropriate colours and high current emissions.

One fact that always perplexed me was the great expense incurred by students in studying chemistry as a practical subject whereas physics students carried out their experiments with minimal investment of their own money. In first- and second-year chemistry classes, a significant financial deposit was required in order to use the thermometers that were essential to obtaining data from many experiments. Physics laboratories also leant heavily on the use of mercury in glass thermometers but there was no student laboratory deposit. I now recall only one occasion on which a thermometer was broken in class and that was believed to have been due directly to the demonstrator using it as a pointer rather than as a measuring instrument. Chemistry classes, on the other hand, were continually being disrupted by the sound of breaking glass and the sight of quicksilver flowing effortlessly over the floor and down the cracks in the parquet flooring. I am sure there was a moral here somewhere but I never quite grasped what it was. Maybe physicists are more confident in their abilities than other scientists.

In the late Forties, it was still impossible to graduate from university prior to the age of twenty-one and, for that reason, students that were ahead of the game at university had to mark time a little in their third or fourth year prior to graduation. A fellow physicist, John Drinkall, and I comprised the only science students taking experimental psychology in year three.

In 1950, it was not yet possible to take psychology to degree level. However, an expanding and lively department headed by George Seth was offering courses that could be taken either in the Faculty of Arts or in the Faculty of Science. As John and I were the first ever students from Science to take the subsidiary course in psychology, part of our laboratory syllabus involved the building of a laboratory for so-called 'psycho-physical method' studies. Psychophysics was an area of study that rather appealed to me at the time. It purported to relate physical stimulus to sensation in a quantitative way. If, for example, a generator of sound was available and the intensity of that sound could be varied in a known way, for example, doubled, trebled, quadrupled, and so on, it was then possible to record the subjective observation of an observer making the judgement as to when precisely the intensity of the sound had doubled, or trebled, quadrupled, and so on. Usually, in such an experiment, the intensity of the source was varied until the sensation registered by the observer was a simple multiple of the original stimulus. Similar experiments, following the work of Stevens at Harvard, related temperature to sensation of coldness or hotness, and just noticeable differences or JNDs could be measured in individual cases indicating the extent to which a stimulus had to be increased for a difference in sensation to be recorded.

John and I were naturally interested in the generation of stimuli as this was closely related to our courses in physics. However, the discovery that sensation, as recorded by an observer, was related logarithmically to the stimulus raised the question as to whether the sensation and the stimulus were indeed different quantities or whether, in estimating the sensation caused by a stimulus, the subject was merely measuring the stimulus in a slightly different way. As we proceeded through the normal lecture course and laboratories involving Rorschach tests, intelligence quotient measurements, and memory tests, we became totally immersed in both the language and the culture of psychology as a discipline at that time. Determining whether one was a behaviourist or a gestältist took quite a lot of time and coffee but was a question that could be discussed by arts and science students alike.

One result of this year of experimental psychology was that I realised the potential for a decatron scaler to assist in the measurement of personal reaction times using the fiftieth of a second unit of counting available from the local mains electricity supply. 'Simple' reaction times in which a subject responds directly to a stimulus, 'choice' where distinction between two alternatives has to be made, and 'discrimination' in which different responses to different stimuli are required varied for most individuals by multiples of a tenth of a second. It was, therefore, possible using the electronics associated with nuclear counting systems to make reaction time measurements of hitherto unknown accuracy. It was some six years later that I realised the measurements made earlier had been at the forefront of experimental techniques in this particular field of study.

There were two colleagues in the honours physics class which I attended that even now stick in my memory but for quite different reasons. The first was John Pringle, who was a congenial colleague and a very hardworking student. It was, therefore, no surprise to find that he had gained a first class honours degree on completion of his course. However, it transpired that just prior to his graduation an uncle died overseas and left a considerable amount of money to John on the understanding that he would become a practising barrister. For this to occur, John had to immediately replace his physics books with law books, enrol for a law degree, and return to the rigours of in-depth study from which he had only just surfaced through graduation. My recollection is that he completed his law degree more than successfully, attaining the only first class honours degree awarded in that subject for a decade.

Another friend, Peter McNeil, was a very large man and he rode to class each day on a large, very large, bicycle. It had large wheels, a large frame, and few, if any, gears but seemed to do the job for Peter. Each day he would ride in and lean his bicycle against the steps leading up to the physics department, forget about it all day, and then reclaim it at the commencement of his journey home. Towards the end of our degree course, Professor Emeleus became concerned that someone might in fact steal Peter's bicycle and, with that in mind, he talked to my friend and suggested that he buy a combination lock of some kind to ensure that his form of transportation was not denied to him through theft. For some weeks, the bicycle was judiciously parked and a sophisticated combination lock affixed to it but, just when this problem ceased to occupy everyone's mind, Peter was somewhat astonished to discover that whereas his bicycle was still at the foot of the steps at the end of a day's work, the expensive combination lock appeared to have gone. It seems that the safety mechanism had more appeal than the rusty mass of steel and rubber that was the McNeil workhorse. A replacement for the missing lock was never purchased and we were never deprived of the fine sight of McNeil cycling home in full cry.

As the class moved inexorably forward towards completion of the honours degree in physics, the students became more aware of the opportunities and features of physics elsewhere in the world. In particular, a close working relationship seemed to exist between Queen's University, Belfast, and Queen's University at Kingston in Canada insofar as the physics departments at both universities were concerned. My final-year laboratory instructor, Brian Love, then a graduate student, moved to Kingston to join his brother, Maurice, who had held a faculty appointment there for some time. There were also presentations from visiting lecturers who had crossed the pond from Canada to cement the linkages already mentioned.

Students in the final-year undergraduate laboratory class normally worked in pairs and I was fortunate to have as my partner, Brian Wilson, who ended up at the University of Calgary in Alberta sometime before I translated myself through England to the University of Manitoba in Winnipeg. Brian obtained his PhD at the Institute for Advanced Studies in Dublin and then helped to establish the Sulfur Mountain Neutron Monitor in Calgary which has been a source of scientific data for around thirty years. Brian Wilson is currently the vice-chancellor of the University of Queensland in Brisbane.

When we worked together in our final year of undergraduate physics at Queen's University, Belfast, Brian, who was a very accomplished hockey player, would occasionally be competing for the university in competitions elsewhere in Ireland or the United Kingdom. On one such occasion I was left to carry out the famous Millikan Oil-Drop experiment on my own and was doing it confidently as the theory was very well understood by all of us and the experiment, in many ways, appeared childishly simple. The idea behind this project is that an individual oil drop, charged by friction in an atomiser, is allowed to fall between two parallel metal plates and be viewed by a telescope mounted at right angles to the fall of the drop. The drops are illuminated by a horizontal light and the little beauties shine like stars as they fall. An electrical voltage applied between the two plates can, however, cause the falling oil drop to cease its motion and even move upwards in the opposite direction to its original fall. Continual studies of such drops falling under gravity and later returning to their original positions enables the elementary charge on the electron to be measured with accuracy and certainty.

Unfortunately, in order to focus the telescope on the central region of the volume under study, it is necessary first to focus the telescope on an object temporarily placed in that position. Normally the oil drops enter through a pinhole in the upper metal plate and it is customary for focusing purposes to place a pin between the plates and then use it as an object upon which to focus the instrument. Refusing any help or assistance from either instructor or graduate student, I happily placed the pin in position and focused the instrument, but omitted to remove the pin. When I applied the voltage between the electrical plates I then, of course, managed to short circuit the system; the pin melted and adhered itself semi-permanently to both the upper and lower plates. I suppose it took me two afternoons to complete the experiment if I discount the three days in which I struggled to remove the residue of the pin and deposits of molten metal from all sides of the experimental chamber. As Robert Andrew Millikan was awarded the Nobel Prize in Physics in 1923 for this experiment, I was probably a candidate for the Ignobel Prize in the same subject in 1952.

It is a strange fact of life that one is always looking forward to a good time ahead. The view of high school from junior school is a rosy one. The anticipation of attaining university is a great incentive for most and graduation is a threshold leading to a lifetime of work either as a professional scientist, a teacher, a businessman, or industrialist. Because of the intensive study required for success and the rapid succession of deadlines to be met on the way, the moments in which success can be savoured are few but precious. There is a camaraderie, a unity of purpose, and an optimism about a graduating class that exists for only a moment before important and increasingly vital decisions are to be made in respect of every student's future. Happiness is a difficult sensation to quantify, but for just one moment and perhaps only one day as we graduated from Queen's University, Belfast, the class of 1952 felt that industry had, for the moment, found its own reward.

Chapter Three

The Physicist as a Graduate Student

The decision to continue in academic study arises inexorably from small beginnings. The seeds of graduate study are sown in the late stages of undergraduate discovery. New skills hold keys to magic casements, and regular if remote contact with sleepless, semi-starving demigods, as all graduate students at that time seem to be, sparks the flames of tireless inquiry that become an all-consuming passion in the future.

Initially, however, my transition to graduate study was fraught with uncertainty. Graduate students in physics at Queen's University generally worked in the basement of the physics building on problems concerning gas discharges and optical phenomena. That field had never, despite the exhortations of the department head, appealed to me. I had a distinct feeling that many of the discoveries made by university researchers in that area had long been known to industrial giants such as Phillips and Ferranti. However, fortunately for me and coincident with my time of decision, a young, intelligent and enthusiastic lecturer in physics arrived from University College, London, full of the joys of analytical and numerical calculation of atomic collision processes. This single fact opened up my career in a new and unanticipated direction – theoretical physics.

I vividly recall meeting with Brian Bransden for the first time in June 1952 and accepting his advice to read and enjoy Mott and Massey's marvellous book *The Theory of Atomic Collisions* over the summer. That modest request from my soon-to-be supervisor effectively changed my life in an instant. Indeed, I and a second student called Marshall King became overnight the first two research students in theoretical physics that the department had ever known. The impact on other researchers was not inconsiderable.

Firstly, a new 'laboratory' within which we would work had to be found. Secondly, because this designated area finally transpired to be the turret room of the University Western Tower, a means of communication with our supervisor, located in the main physics building one hundred metres and a myriad stone steps of spiral staircase away, had to be created.

The latter presented quite a challenge, but one which we solved with both effectiveness and elegance. In the physics museum were several ancient telephones of great craftsmanship and quality. They were magneto-driven, each with a handle that was turned rapidly to electrify the line. Our first task was to lay telephone line from the tower along the rafters of several teaching laboratories and eventually terminate it at Dr Bransden's office. The excitement with which the first call from this Neolithic communications system was received was a triumph of huge dimensions for two raw students of theoretical physics. The system worked.

The turret room in which we were now finally ensconced had, unknown to us, featured in a detective novel entitled *The Weight of Evidence* by the redoubtable Michael Innes. Innes, whose real name was J.I.M. Stewart (John Innes Macintosh), had been a lecturer in the English department at Queen's University and was quite a prolific writer of fiction.

In this particular novel, a professor of history reclining in a chaise longue or similar article of quadrangle furniture is struck and killed by a meteorite which either came from the heavens as an act of God or from the tower as an act of villainy. Fortunately, King and McKee were not residents of the upper tower at the time, but the tale added spice and a *je ne sais quoi* to our studies throughout the PhD research programme. In fact, we both found the conditions under which we thought, discussed and calculated, conducive to such actions. The working day was interrupted only by prearranged visits to or from our supervisor and precisely timed trips to the students union or refectory for coffee, tea or lunch.

On one such occasion an event, however, did occur which was to have some influence on later developments. In order to appreciate what transpired, a few words about the head of the department, Professor Karl G. Emeleus, are necessary at this point. Professor Emeleus was a quiet, unassuming, generally mild man of a light and wiry form. He was naturally soft spoken, and gave his lectures, which were superbly precise and logical in style, a penetrating quality that compelled the listener to attend to every word. On those rare occasions on which a first-year class of a hundred or so students would create noise or disturbance of any kind, Emeleus would simply continue his lecture while speaking even more softly and clearly than usual. As a result, you could literally hear a pin drop in any classes which he personally taught.

At the graduate student level, however, he was somewhat remote from most of the students apart from those working directly with him. It was always said that he had two great ambitions. The first was to become a fellow of the Royal Society (his brother, a chemist, had already received that distinction), and the second to make a century in any class of cricket. For that reason the annual staff/student cricket match assumed an importance not usually attributed to such an event. To my understanding the great cricketing ambition was never achieved despite determined efforts on everyone's part to meet that end. His appreciation of cricket and cricketers was, however, evident on an everyday basis.

My friend, Herbie Martin, research student and opening bat for Ireland, used to be actively discouraged from carrying out experimental work in his Faraday cage in the basement on the day prior to any international tourney, as Emeleus felt the dark environment could adversely affect Martin's performance in the brighter light of game day. Others of us who lacked Herbie's natural talent were never to find an excuse to cease and desist from pounding our Marchant electric calculators, or taking experimental data, whether game day or otherwise.

Perhaps my most vivid recollection of Professor Emeleus as I write this chapter is of my summons to his home in Dunmurry for coffee and dessert one evening while in the second year of my doctoral studies. At the time I was very active in student politics being immediate past president of the students representative council, vice-president of the National Union of Students (England, Wales and Northern Ireland) and an enthusiastic if not brilliant field hockey player. After coffee it transpired that my date with 'the boss' was not of a wholly social nature. It seemed that my supervisor, Brian Bransden, was to move on to higher things, namely a professorship at Glasgow where I would be required to go also from time to time for consultations. More importantly there would now be, within the Department of Physics, a dearth of people to teach theoretical electricity. The master plan thus was for me to take over the responsibility for this course, starting the following Monday, and to assume the rank of assistant lecturer with faculty status attached.

The rest of the evening was then devoted to laying on the line the implications of my sudden promotion while still a student. I must make no more student friendships. I should take no further part in local student politics, and of course playing on university hockey teams while also an instructor would place me in an impossible conflict of interest situation in addition to being inappropriate for a faculty member.

Never having heard such nonsensical instructions given by one academic to, as it now appeared, another, I instinctively agreed to all demands and then went on my way rejoicing and to tell my present and continuing friends the epic news. The general idea that one could not be a professional scientist and teacher while maintaining existing friendships with fellow students seemed incredible to me. However, it was my undergraduate friends, including Phil Stevenson, the captain of the university first XI hockey team, who made my transition to academic ranks a smooth if not entirely uneventful one.

I recall, in particular, a few minutes before the start of my first lecture to the third-year class, coming into the lecture theatre to a clamour of noise, hoots and greetings of various kinds. Then a sudden voice – it was Phil shouting, 'Okay fellows, fags out, Jasper is about to start.' That lecture and all that followed that year involved continuing interaction between the class and the raw lecturer.

Why use white chalk when the yellow is more readily seen? Why do you adopt the fencing approach to lecturing – thrusting towards the board with the chalk and then withdrawing rapidly? In this way, over a period of two years, I acquired techniques and skills that were to be of great value to me in the Universities of Birmingham and Manitoba later on.

The class in theoretical electricity contained about a hundred students and met at a regularly established time on

Monday, Wednesday and Friday. One day, some two months after my elevation to the teaching staff, Emeleus sent me a note to say that a special event of a cultural nature was taking place coincident with my Wednesday lecture, and that I might consider rescheduling it or alternatively giving it twice! I decided to give my lecture as usual because all the students I spoke to preferred it that way, but also announced that I would repeat the lecture at 5 p.m. that day for anyone missing the earlier performance. It transpired that all but one of the class attended at the usual time, the one being none other than the daughter of the head of department. This was the first and only occasion on which I lectured for one hour to one student in any subject and was an experience so bizarre that I have not wished to repeat it. The young woman, unperturbed, sat in the middle of the theatre and endeavoured to make my task as normal a lecture as could be expected under the circumstances.

Emeleus was however, when all is said and done, a kind man, good to his students while exhibiting a variety of eccentricities, a feature not uncommon to others in academic circles. On a particular occasion towards the end of my time at Queen's he became somewhat obsessed with a fear of burglars breaking into the department and stealing things, though what they could steal of value was likely to be moderate at best. Signs posted around the department stating that 'Faraday did it on less' were a continual reminder that money was unlikely to be thrown at research problems in physics at the best of times.

Then one evening, late in my research student days, I went down into the basement to drag my friend Herbie Martin off for a coffee break at around nine in the evening. Drifting through the various pillars that were a feature of the basement decor I was frightened almost out of my wits by the sudden appearance of a brilliant light in my face and a cry of 'What do you think you are doing here?' It took me a moment to realise that this was the department head, and he even longer to appreciate that I was a research student in physics called McKee who worked in the eerie fastness of the physics tower. At this time, according to my colleagues who worked in the basement, it was not unusual for Professor Emeleus to hide, torch in hand, behind a pillar, from which he might leap out and attempt to apprehend robbers at any time. The good news concerning this encounter was that Emeleus then escorted me apologetically to his study, where for the first time since enrolling as a graduate student I had the opportunity to discuss with him in detail the research that I was doing, and my future career and opportunities. He was, as I said, an eccentric but a kind and helpful man.

The one encounter with him which I will never forget took place in the early spring of 1954. Marshall King and I had trooped down to the Students Union cafeteria for our customary coffee break at 10.30 a.m. Sitting as I was at an extreme corner of the table I proved a ready receptacle for the contents of two cups of coffee deposited by a young woman student on collision with a friend. Being soused from thigh to foot with this warmer than normal liquid I immediately returned to the tower room where I removed and washed my trousers and hung them out of a window on the side away from the quadrangle and over the Botanical Gardens which are adjacent to the university. Having little else to do I returned to my normal computing tasks clad tastefully in my Y-fronts, but little else. Some ten minutes after my resumption of work I heard a footfall or two on the spiral staircase leading to the tower room door. Anticipating Marshall's return, I barely noticed the door opening and two people entering, one being Professor Emeleus, our esteemed department head.

'Mr McKee,' said Emeleus, 'I would like to introduce you to the head of our sister department in Sydney, Australia, who I thought would appreciate the view from this tower.'

My horrified response was merely, 'Pleased to meet you sir, but I have no trousers on.'

To which Emeleus responded without hesitation, 'That is all right, McKee, please don't trouble to get up.'

The visitor's gaze was then directed to a variety of local landmarks – including the Botanical Gardens – and then both left, apologising for the interruption of my studies.

From that day to this the matter was never raised by either Emeleus or myself. However, some weeks later, Herbie Martin confided in me that Emeleus remarked to him one evening that perhaps the theoretical physicists in the tower were too remote from the activities of the rest of the department. Shortly after, Marshall King graduated and went across to AERE Harwell where he had a most successful career, and I was given my own room in a newly acquired property in University Square. This time roughly corresponded with my elevation to the ranks of the academic staff.

Further recollections of my period as a graduate student in physics are few, apart from the years when I was also president of the Students Representative Council, which will be referred to elsewhere. This period as president was prior to my lecturing appointment, and was responsible for extending my period of study for the PhD degree by about nine months. But to return to the highlights of my early days in graduate school.

There are certainly two that spring to mind, the first concerning my acquisition of a research studentship in open competition, which covered most of my expenses for three years of study, and the second an act of initiation into the ranks of graduate students which will demonstrate how gullible even research physicists can be, on occasion.

When Brian Bransden first encouraged me to apply for the studentship I did so, but with some apprehension. The all-faculty committee included representatives from the sciences, but neither my supervisor nor department head were present, and the challenge of communicating a research project in theoretical physics to an essentially non-scientific panel was considerable. Nevertheless, following my supervisor's instructions, I explained to the committee that one of the foremost problems of the time in nuclear physics – a new field – was to understand the scattering of neutrons by alpha particles at low energies, and the possible existence of states of helium-five, as the resulting system of neutron and alpha particle was called. A recent calculation by a physicist called Nogami in Japan had indicated that the sign of the S-wave phase shift in this scattering process was negative, but we had reasons to believe that this deduction was incorrect. My first task was therefore to confirm, or otherwise, the Japanese result, before tackling the sterner tasks ahead. There was a somewhat protracted silence following my presentation, after which the committee chair thanked me for my remarks and looked helplessly for questions from the rest of the committee. These when they were offered were largely trivial – why was I interested in collision theory? Was I a mathematician or a physicist? Did I think my career so far had equipped me to tackle such a demanding field? My confidence was now substantial.

'Any further questions?' asked the chair.

The Professor of History put up his hand, 'Perhaps I may clarify a point? McKee, you say you wish to repeat and refine a Japanese piece of work – do you read Japanese?'

'No, sir.'

'Is Nogami's work largely published in his native tongue in the first instance?'

'Yes, sir!'

'How then can you believe that there is actually a problem that requires solution?'

At this point I wished the earth to open up and swallow me. I could not say, 'My supervisor told me so,' as that would have been game, set and match. I paused for what seemed an eternity before, in a rare fit of inspiration, I responded, 'As you will be aware, mathematical physics is largely mathematics and fortunately mathematics is the same in any language. Normally, however, your point would be well taken, sir.' At this point I knew I would be successful. I still have the impression that few faculty members, quite apart from students, ever got one over on the Professor of History. Their delight at my answer was, I feel, no less than mine.

After the interview was over, I ran to the library to look up the original source of the work which I described. There was rather more text than mathematics, but fortunately nothing to cast doubt on my confident assessment of the situation. So we progress.

The pursuit of research in physics involves total commitment and provides less opportunity for mingling than most career paths. As a graduate student my research work was all-consuming apart from statutory breaks such as afternoon tea in the lecture-preparation room where everyone would assemble at around 4 p.m. Tea was made by students in rotation and served from the Elizabeth Joy Williamson memorial teapot. The pot was immense and must have held several litres of liquid – perhaps it held an imperial gallon, I do not know. Certainly, it was believed to have been constructed by a graduate student as part of her technical and practical training, although who she was and how she had fared in her studies were never discussed.

On my second official day as a fully-fledged research student, I was having tea when one of the senior fellows mentioned that although I was now a graduate student it was up to me to show that I had the necessary qualities of physical science understanding and co-ordination in order to succeed in a PhD research programme. To that end I was required to stand erect with head tilted back and balance a sixpence (a small British coin, something the size of a dime) on the centre of my forehead. At this point a glass filter funnel was stuck into the waistband of my pants as centrally as possible so that I might tilt my head forward, slide the coin down my nose, and invoke gravity to transport it into the funnel. I was allowed two tries prior to the real thing. Needless to say, the task proved impossible, but on each try I was assured that tilting my head further back and coming forward more slowly was all that was required. I can still recall vividly the moment of the third try. Just as I was about to tilt my head forward a chilling numbness attacked my nether regions, and all pretext at real competition was gone. Those insufferable idiots, my new companions, had waited until all conditions were perfect before pouring a flask of ether down the filter funnel and in and around man's chief end and accessories.

That it took me some time to thaw out, and that the effect was transitory is the good news. The better news is that I personally would never have to endure the challenge again. Not that this initiation rite would not recur in many different but similar situations. It did. But no occasion could equal the initiation of Thong Saw Pak.

Thong had arrived as a visiting researcher from Malaysia for a summer as I now recall the incident, and like all other newcomers, the tea club informed him of its novel test for scientific ability and technical skill. Obligingly, Thong, who was stocky of build but not overly tall attempted very seriously to catch the sixpence in the funnel firmly ensconced in his trousers belt. On the third try, while he was leaning far back and concentrating valiantly, a senior member of the club poured the previously concealed ether down the funnel and inside his pants as the custom dictated. Immediately, however, it was as if a devil was unleashed. Thong took the nearest two students, one in each hand, and carried them out of the building and on to the grass outside where he banged them together. Such a show of strength and controlled anger had never before been seen by the tea club. What the rest of us did not know, but presumably the head of department did, was that Thong Saw Pak had recently competed as a weightlifter at the Helsinki Olympic Games, a qualification regarded as of little significance compared with his abilities as a physicist. Thong later became the Chair of Physics at the Research Institute in Ipoh, Malaysia. He was, in fact, a charming and gentle man. Shortly after this time, and perhaps as a result of the incident, the initiation rite was discontinued and the hazards of tea drinking greatly reduced.

One final recollection of those two early years as a graduate student while Marshall King and I resided in our lofty tower was the inability of the department head to distinguish between us, despite the fact that I was over six feet one inch tall and Marshall was an athletic and wiry five feet eight. The greeting from Professor Emeleus at colloquia or passing on stairs was invariably 'Good morning, King... or is it McKee?' or the alternative with the names reversed. Only after Marshall's departure and my appointment as assistant lecturer did this distinct ambiguity become clearly resolved, although the earlier incident in the tower room must have gone a long way towards identifying McKee... or is it King?

Chapter Four

The Physicist Discovers Local Politics

Both my immediate and extended family members in Northern Ireland were politically and unthinkingly Conservative. That is to say, they always voted Ulster Unionist at election time and never even remotely considered any other political possibility. In their minds, union with Britain was the only option consistent with past history and economic promise, and that being the case nationalist, Hibernian and other candidates were totally anathema to them. Other options came and went with time, but no party other than the Conservative and Unionist party was unequivocal about the position of Northern Ireland as an integral component of the United Kingdom, and that, in essence, was that.

The fact that time in Ulster had stood still for some two and a half centuries prior to this period did not seem to be notable or relevant to this particular twentieth century electorate. The fact that King William of Orange had defeated the Catholic pretender James II at the Battle of the Boyne in 1690 was the only pertinent detail to be considered.

Local economic problems, discrimination in the job market, and in many cases outright bigotry in the work force, were never election issues in the normal political sense. The events of 1690 determined voting preferences in 1950, and it seemed that nothing could be done to change the immutable situation. But, despite the apparent inevitability of Conservative-Unionist success at election time, a new generation of Ulster men and women, my peers and contemporaries, managed to develop a deep and healthy scepticism in relation to much of the basis of traditional thought. Why were social and economic issues not the substance of an election platform? we asked. Why were so many colourless, incompetent and virtually inanimate members elected time after time to sit silent for years on the government back benches at Westminster and Stormont?

In particular, my local Belfast constituency in Northern Ireland elections boasted a perpetual incumbent, a retired lieutenant-colonel with a significant war record, who conducted a very straightforward if simplistic election campaign on each occasion. He rode on a white horse through every street in the electorate, speaking and stopping rarely, if ever, but reminding everyone that the politics of 1690 were still the politics of the day. The crossing of the Boyne by King William on a white horse over two centuries previously was re-enacted as a continuous sign and symbol of the supremacy and control of the Conservative and Unionist Party in Northern Ireland.

The situation was bizarre, to say the least. To me, this method of seeking re-election to either house, whether Stormont or Westminster seemed such an insult to the intelligence of voters that I resolved to try to find a better alternative for my support, a progressive party, and hopefully, a candidate. To be disillusioned with politics before you reach voting age, is of course a frustrating state of affairs, to say the least. That, however, was precisely my situation on leaving high school.

It was accordingly, therefore, a great delight to discover, on my arrival at Queen's University as a raw and hapless undergraduate, that there were, in fact, other and developing options on the horizon that could perhaps change the face of politics in Ulster. It was in anticipation and hope that I joined the serried ranks of the Liberal Association of Queen's University Belfast at my earliest opportunity, a step which did much to shape my philosophy and thought in later stages of my academic career.

Shortly after, in 1953, I became chairman of the Queen's University Liberal Association, succeeding a splendidly traditional Liberal with the classic Welsh name of Davis, whose father had actually known Lloyd George, and whose roots were firmly established in post-Gladstonian Liberalism. The lively and enthusiastic association that he had developed, grew rapidly during my year as chair, due largely to the support of liberal democrats in the United States and the free supply of films and documentaries of a political nature from both the local consulate and the United States embassy in London.

We were a sociable and active group and managed to amass a membership in excess of three hundred and sixty-five souls, or one for each day of the calendar year. Though many members were associated for overtly social reasons and many others were only mildly political, the group became the largest university political group in the United Kingdom, despite the fact that no liberal party as such existed at that time in Northern Ireland.

This particular situation, however, was shortly remedied when, concurrent with the success of the University Liberal Association, a second largely non-university group finally established a Northern Ireland Liberal Party with electoral aspirations. Almost immediately, when an eagerly anticipated provincial election was called, a lawyer and alumnus of the university, Sheelagh Murnaghan, was elected to take the first Liberal seat in the Northern Ireland Parliament at Stormont, as a university member. With an elected member in Parliament, the political future of liberalism in the province suddenly looked bright, but the brightness was largely illusory.

In coincidence with the birth of the Liberal Party in Northern Ireland, I resigned my position as chair of the Liberal Association at the university. The reason for this sudden political volte-face was that I had been persuaded that my experience and services were needed as the next president of the Students Representative Council, the governing body for student affairs at the university.

To stand for such office it was necessary to be apolitical and not overtly involved with any political party. So, shortly after my resignation, I was overwhelmingly elected president of the SRC for the year 1953–1954, the second year of my graduate studies. Towards the end of my year of service as president, I became an assistant lecturer in physics, and automatically translated from student politician to academic extraordinaire. Nonetheless, the brief but fascinating year as president was to lead to further advancement in the arena of student politics despite my newly acquired academic status. My election to the national executive of the National Union of Students at its annual congress was followed one year later by election to the position of deputy president in 1955–1956, an office which I finally relinquished at the annual congress in Birmingham in the autumn of the year. This period with the NUS, then the ninth largest union in Britain, was one which was to launch me on the international scene both as a student leader and as an embryonic academic. It is therefore important to review some of the more memorable features of student politics both in Northern Ireland and abroad in the years 1954 to 1956.

The problem of Unionism, that is to say the union of Northern Ireland with Great Britain, was now to become no less a problem for the Liberals than for members of any other opposition party. Being 'soft on the rebels', as many would imaginatively describe the Liberal position on Unionism, forced Liberal Unionists back into the clutches of the Tory Party. My view, which in general terms was that of the Liberal Party, visualised the maintenance of union with Britain as a permanent policy until such time as a majority of the population in the North wished for change. This typically liberal solution to the problem was, however, perceived as disguising the real intentions of the party, namely to dissolve the British link at the earliest possible opportunity. That such was not the case could not be readily demonstrated, and so the Liberal Party became lost in the political wilderness, along with all those who did not have an unequivocal position on the Unionist question. Unionist first and Conservative second was the posture of the Tory Party, and even when Terence O'Neil, later Lord O'Neil, was almost able (some years later) to demonstrate that the border between Ulster and the Republic was becoming an obstacle to economic progress, the traditional ranks of Unionism reformed, and the rest is contemporary history.

Despite the changing political climate in Northern Ireland and increasing political activism, there were no significant acts of violence on the Queen's University campus during my eight-year sojourn there. Admittedly there was the one occasion on which an errant snowball removed a policeman's helmet while he was patrolling the hallowed grounds of the university. A major incident was however narrowly averted when it was established that the officer was present on campus without invitation and therefore *persona non grata*. The incident was then quickly defused. Of more lasting and perhaps political significance was the riot following a debate on the subject of 'This house believes in monarchy', held, I believe, in the spring of 1954.

It was always the custom at Queen's to hold an annual 'orange and green' debate at which Nationalist and Unionist orators could strut their stuff and two thousand vocal students let off the steam that centuries of ill-remembered history had generated. The organising body was always the Literific, the Literary and Scientific Society, that could boast most of the Western world's literary and political figures as speakers on its roster at one time or another. On this particular occasion the proposer of the motion that 'This house believes in monarchy' was none other than 'The O'Brien, Earl of Thomond' and rightful heir (according to him) to the historic throne of Ireland.

Now to say that O'Brien was a crank and a deceiver would be to underestimate his performance and background. He dressed and looked every inch a king from his cutaway waistcoat or vest to his ceremonial sword. He produced documentation that indicated the support of outer Mongolia and the Philippines for his claim to the monarchy – a claim which he assured the audience was currently before the United Nations for full consideration. His analysis of the need for, and benefits of monarchy was logical and thoughtful. The idea of a powerless figurehead as a uniting force for public good was unfortunately, however, a little too much for the audience to accept and the debate deteriorated rapidly with time.

Precisely how the riot occurred is now lost in the mists of history. It appears that suddenly most of the Republicans present could take no more of the O'Brien argument and I suspect the Unionists, more confused than anything else, felt similarly moved. As a result war broke out. Tables were overturned and used as shields, and the audience began throwing everything within sight at the heroic figure of

O'Brien and his protecting hosts on the organising committee. With a mob of two thousand souls engaged in hand to hand warfare, the protection of the guest became paramount and difficult to assure. This is where I came in. As president of the Students Representative Council and vice-president of the Students Union, I was entrusted with the task of arranging for and getting O'Brien to the getaway car, a task which would not prove simple. Initially, we got him to the safe confines of the student offices where he calmly awaited the escape vehicle. This occurred, as luck would have it, just as the offices were finally surrounded and cut off from the outside world. Simultaneously, the pickup car appeared outside and somehow or other O'Brien was secreted out of a small window, then fled across the road and finally was off in the waiting vehicle seconds later. In retrospect, the debate was both a challenging and comical event, but one that those fortunate enough to attend still recall with clarity and some admiration. O'Brien was, as the Canadians say, 'something else'.

Some months later several members of the Students Union Committee were invited to Thomond Castle to receive from the king-apparent the honour of a knighthood and to become knights of the Order of Thomond. I thought the whole thing quite silly at the time and declined the offer, but several of the officers of the Students Union accepted the honour. They went down to Limerick and walked the red carpet in Thomond Castle, to be dubbed as knights by O'Brien. My wife and daughter never forgave me for my failure to accept the offer which would have meant much to them. Sir Jasper is one thing, but Lady Christine would have had a pleasant ring to it.

Chapter Five

The Physicist as a Journalist and Observer of Our Times

Journalism is a career into which it is best to be projected rather than to aspire. It was never clear to me why I, a dedicated physics student, was invited to don the mantle of Queensman with his two hundred anonymous words per week in the *Belfast Newsletter*, or later the role of Alumnus in the *Belfast Telegraph*. In the end, however, it took a mere two months of writing both sets of articles simultaneously for a discerning public to determine that the style, or lack of it, of both contributions was essentially the same, and immediately phase one of my journalistic career was over.

Communicating effectively within the confines of two hundred words is a daunting and useful challenge, particularly for an Irishman, coming as I did from a tradition that considers the use of one word, when twenty-three will do equally well, totally reprehensible. The effort to comply was Herculean. Nonetheless, searching for items of news from the university likely to interest a diverse public outside was a fascinating business, and one of great value to me in later life.

In the summer of 1954, at approximately the time when my dual aliases were finally discovered, I was given the opportunity to visit Greece for an extended period. As vice-president of the National Union of Students I was to carry greetings and best wishes for the success of the newly formed Greek Union comprising the two Universities of Athens and Thessalonika. This union was consummated at a banquet in the Pantheon Hotel in Athens and as an exercise in international co-operation was a resounding success and a fine example. However, prior to my departure for Greece I had a short interview with the 'younger' Mr Henderson, proprietor of the *Belfast Newsletter*, who indicated that his newspaper would pay for two or three travel articles covering my journey and would consider others if regarded as newsworthy or different. In particular he gave me distinct instructions as to how to address such material. Whenever you arrive in a new country, town or place always note down your first impressions immediately. What do the people look like – are they different? In what way? What about the houses, are they like Irish or English houses? Do they have window shutters? Are they coloured or plain? If coloured, are they all different or all the same? Questions such as these only arise on first arrival. The second day they and you become part of the scene. You observe by noting contrast. Do it at once, or the message you need to convey will be missed.

So, with this monologue as background, I travelled hopefully and confidently to Greece. The stay in Athens was fairly short. Accommodation in the student hostel several kilometres from Omonia Square was adequate, and the climate everything to be desired from an Irishman's point of view. The mountains behind the city, dominated at the most visible point by Mad Emitos were enfolded by an endless sky of the deepest blue. While waiting for the celebrations of union at week's end my colleagues and I visited all the essential features of the city from the Acropolis through the Agora and the Plaka to the Temple of Zeus. At this time the destruction of ancient structures by acid gases from uncontrolled vehicle emissions had barely become noticeable. The dramatically-painted resistance symbol 'oxi' was still visible on the mountain range, a last remnant of the Second World War.

The location of the student hostel initially caused something of a problem. Having been escorted there by our student hosts, the task of finding it again seemed trivial in the extreme, especially as I had learned to commit to paper everything likely to be useful during my travels. It was therefore natural for me to write down the address of the hostel which was distinctly visible on a plate at the corner of the building.

When my friend Rob and I had spent the evening eating and drinking in downtown Athens, our return seemed simple enough. Get a bus from Omonia Square with the same number as that which delivered us there, go to the conductor/driver and indicate that two tickets are required, either through the use of two fingers, the word *dio*, or both, and then display the piece of paper showing our destination. Well, we did all that, with no expectation of the actual result. The driver started laughing, first moderately and then uncontainably. He stopped the bus, stood up and addressed the passengers who to a person burst into uncontrollable paroxysms of mirth. Fortunately for us, there was one passenger who had at one stage fought with the Northumberland Fusiliers, and understood and spoke English perfectly. It was he who broke the news that we had requested two tickets to 'spitting not allowed'! Nothing anyone could suggest would now direct us to our destination. We left the bus almost immediately, and walked most of the bus route in the dark trying to find a plaque similar to our original inspiration. We did succeed, but only after two hours of the blind leading the blind and with the pitiless laughter of a busload of Athenians ringing in our ears.

With two days to go before the Pantheon event, a colleague and I decided to visit Delphi and consult the oracle, in as far as that is possible in these days of harsh reality. Travelling by bus was and is a terrifying experience to the unsuspecting. Sheer cliffs on one side of the road with fast-moving traffic driving only on the strength of their horns, with no fences and no dividers seemed a recipe for disaster, and apparently such disasters were not infrequent. Rounding Mount Helicon at speed left little time or inclination to reflect on mythology. Only on arrival at Delphi was it possible to reflect peacefully on the ancient history of the area and see, as the gods must have done, the eagles swooping round the bulk of Mount Parnassus.

Open air cafés and the clarion sounds of bazoukis are my lasting memories of night in Delphi. Walking from there to Itea on the gulf of Corinth in siesta time, through the olive groves, with a swim in the gulf as a reward, completed a brief sortie into the Greece of my early history texts. So back to Athens.

The affair at the Pantheon Hotel was warm and historic. The greetings from the National Union of Students of England, Wales and Northern Ireland were received enthusiastically, as were a few student anecdotes appropriate perhaps to such a festivity. Once this evening was over, my responsibilities had in principle come to an end, but that was not to be. Firstly, the newly created Union saw fit to present Queen's University Students Representative Council with an urn of majestic proportions, so majestic in fact that bringing it home was a challenge of the first magnitude. Travelling as I was, deck class on a ship to Brindisi and then third class on a European train, sea ferry to England, rail to Liverpool and then by sea to Ireland, the future of the artefact was always in doubt. However, despite many instances which might have proved disastrous to the future of the Grecian urn, I was able to present it to my home university as an unsolicited gift from the Universities of Athens and Thessalonika. The fact that a cleaning person removed it from the trophy cabinet to clean it several months later and dropped it, cannot detract from the Herculean effort required in giving her the eventual opportunity.

The second unexpected event was one of unusual significance. While still staying in the youth hostel, a message was sent from a member of the Students Union Committee to indicate that an invitation to coffee had come to me from a well-known Athenian lawyer, Dr Socrates Loizides, whose chambers were at 11 Homer Street, and would I accept? Not wishing to appear churlish I responded that I would, and this is where things immediately became interesting. At that time, the Enossis Movement directed towards uniting Cyprus with Greece was in its infancy. Dr Loizides, later to be nicknamed 'the snake', was an influential leader of the movement. He had heard somehow of my visit, and believed that because I was from the North of Ireland, itself the subject of continued dispute between two countries, my appreciation of the Cyprus problem might be more acute than the next person's. In addition I was representing the ninth largest union in the United Kingdom and was a student leader – students being traditionally the radical influence in politics in Europe. What he did not know was that I was also a freelance journalist, and from my point of view, the meeting as it unfolded could not have been more valuable. Over coffee, he first gave me an overview of the history of Cyprus, of the conflict between Greece and Turkey and of the claims of Greece on the island itself. Makarios, Eoka and the drawing of lines of demarcation were largely for the future. The case for Enossis was however new to people in Britain and Ireland, and it was my opportunity to be able to publish in the *Belfast Newsletter* the account of my interview with

Loizides, as a bonus to my other journalistic commitments. It transpired that this article was the first of its kind in a British newspaper. It was copied and translated for publication in the leading Athens newspapers. The article was written in a question and answer factual interview style, and the topic was of considerable political interest at the time.

On completion of the formal responsibilities I had in Athens, the urn was left in safe keeping for a week while I made an excursion deck class by ship to Rhodos, that beautiful island in the eastern Mediterranean.

Greece had few notable passenger ships in 1954. Most had been acquired from Britain while en route for the knacker's yard, and were of low tonnage, rusted, and internally dilapidated. The exceptions were three vessels obtained from Italy as reparations at the end of the war, renamed as the *Ajax*, *Achilles* and *Agamemnon*. I sailed on none of these. The three thousand five hundred tonne island ferry to Rhodos was far from a luxury vessel and I considered myself fortunate to be confined to the deck. Sleeping below deck was apparently an almost impossible task with the noise of the engines, the heat and the constant vibration enough to keep the dead awake. By day however the vessel steamed through the Cyclades and Sporades with effortless ease and the changing seascape with islands rising from the turquoise waters of the Aegean Sea in every direction made time pass quickly and nothing seem more simple than an eighteen hour sea trip between them.

Tinos, Mykonos, Kos and Kalimnos: all were visited and left behind. Stuccoed houses with blue or red window frames and doors rose in tiers from sea level to hilltop. Schools of dolphins and flying fish would accompany the ship as it plied its inter-island trade. Rhodes, or Rhodos as it is universally called today, has a fine harbour overlooked by the Castle of the Knights of Saint John. As the ship slipped into port it was easy to imagine the ancient colossus standing astride the harbour entrance and looming above you as you made port.

It is difficult now, many years later, to recall clearly the many remarkable features of the city and the island. I remember most vividly the roaring of the crickets in the trees by the roadside, shrill and deafening well into the night. Then there was the mysterious sight of Turkey lying shrouded in heat haze some miles to the east. The valley of butterflies was also beautiful and, if you shouted, a dramatic place. But the finest and most unforgettable feature of the island of Rhodos must be Lindos, an ancient town with its acropolis perched like a seabird's nest – high above the deep blue of the sea – untouched it would seem by the decay becoming noticeable in its better known sister in Athens. Add to this the music that is everywhere, the beautiful Greek food, the remarkable, if simple, churches with their bearded patriarchs, and you have a picture of an island that seemed, certainly in 1954, to resemble paradise.

Of course there were and are some parallels with Cyprus in history and fact. The city of Rhodos has three distinct quarters (or should they be thirds?): a Greek, Turkish and a Jewish quarter; all distinct, and all it would seem living at arm's length from each other. Nonetheless trade and tourism were prospering and perhaps mutual accommodation can work in the right environment.

It would be an understatement to suggest I liked Rhodos. I loved it; it was both lively and beautiful. I liked it so much that I postponed my return to Athens by one day, changing my return ticket from the ship on which I had arrived to a much smaller five hundred tonne ex-British merchant ship which with its sister ship plied continually between the Greek islands carrying people, animals, and produce from one to another. The greatest mistake I ever made was to change my date of departure, but I was not to appreciate that until four hours after leaving port for

Athens. Being deck class I had to buy simple food from a small kiosk as we sailed, in particular a large cheese sandwich and a bottle of retsina – the resinated wine of Greece – to see me through for a day or so. I recall sitting on my sleeping bag by the rail and looking down at the, as it seemed, perpetually calm and blue water.

The storm arose quickly. One moment all was still, the next, deck class folk were rolling all over the deck unless attached firmly to a permanent fixture of the vessel. An old woman helped to tie me to the rails surrounding the deck and there I hung for what seemed an endless night of violent pitching and floods of water. Around midnight an eerie scene took place. A table was brought on deck and lashed to bulwark and mast. Hurricane lanterns were swinging about and it seems that a tourist below deck who had choked on her vomit was being operated on in some way – perhaps a tracheotomy. Whatever the truth of the event, the poor woman, an American I believe, died in the early hours, while the pitching and rolling continued with the vessel making little or no headway. Of course, people who know the Aegean Sea and the Mediterranean Sea well, know that all hell can break loose when the *miltame* blows. It is a wind that at certain times, principally late summer, can funnel down from the Bosphorus and create havoc with sailing and ships as efficiently now as it did in ancient times.

Shortly after daybreak, with the storm still at its height, our vessel made safe harbour in Mykonos as an unscheduled stop. Indeed, the time of our arrival at Mykonos was almost identical to the anticipated time of arrival in the Piraeus, Athens. For several hours we rode out the remainder of the storm. It ceased in mid-morning as suddenly as it had arisen.

Later that evening, under a clear blue sky, upon the most tranquil of water, we finally sailed into port in Athens, the only indication of the horrors behind being the funeral hearse waiting at the dockside for our less fortunate American travelling companion.

Of my final return to university in Belfast, little further need be said. The journey was interminable, the number of people on train and boat uncountable, and comfort non-existent.

Two facts of value were, however, learnt by the traveller. The first was that sleeping overnight on marble in an aesthetically pleasing Italian railroad station does not do much for your bones or your tranquillity; the second that if you are running for a train in Italy and take a quick glance at the train that is leaving, do not think that because 'rapido' is written on the side that it is going to get you anywhere fast. The antithesis is always true. I found this revelation a particularly salutary lesson as I crawled past Rimini and Ancona, stopping at every hole in the hedge or whim of the paying customer.

At home the several two thousand word travel articles that I had been commissioned to write were duly published and attracted more than passing interest. Undoubtedly, however, the interview with Dr Socrates Loizides somewhat overshadowed the previously commissioned works.

On my return, creative journalism was replaced by the hard, objective fact of writing my PhD thesis on the topic of variational methods in collision theory about which little further need be said at this point. Coincident, however, with the completion of the thesis, a further journalistic opportunity arose. I was invited as a member of a small national youth leaders team to visit Berlin and survey the social and political features of that part of Germany in the new post-war era. The time, of course, was interesting because it was prior to the building of the famous Berlin Wall and all movement from eastern to western sector was controlled, if not overly difficult. As deputy president of the National Union of Students at that time and in the absence of the president of the Union, I was nominated to a position among this consortium of school principals, educators, bureaucrats, and other youth leaders. The total number of people involved, I believe, was about half a dozen, but at this stage the precise number is neither easy to recall, nor important. Needless to say, we were shepherded around and protected to some extent by the British Centre, the military body responsible for the activities of visitors to the British sector. An interesting itinerary was prepared for us, embracing our presence at the opening of new high schools, at athletic sports events, attendance at a rock club called the Eirshalle or Egg Shell on one evening, and a visit to the Resibar in downtown Berlin. The Resibar was of particular interest, having a set of fountains at one end which rose, fell and changed colour in time to whatever music was playing. Guests of the establishment sat around tables that were individually numbered. These tables were connected telegraphically, as it were, by a set of copper or brass pipes through which messages in little canisters could be transported by compressed air jet, in a similar way to which change used to be made at major department stores prior to the Second World War. Basically, you put a message in this little canister, closed it up, and pulled a handle. The canister was then whisked to a central control system from which it was then directed to the table of destination. The idea here was that if you looked round the many tables and saw anyone that particularly tickled your fancy, you might engage in a remote conversation through the means of this conveyor system and say, for example, 'I am Joe Blog. Haven't I seen you somewhere before?' and sitting in the security of your position at table twenty-two, you would then actually see the canister arriving at the other table. You would perhaps see directly the response that the message received and then you might await, in tentative anticipation of a reply saying either 'get lost' or 'how interesting to see you again'. After several courses of dinner, a few bottles of wine, and this and that, you might even have the opportunity to dance with an appropriate contact elsewhere in the Resibar. The extent to which this system was activated or actually worked was not clear, but the presence of James Mason, the well-known British actor, at the next table did much to make it a memorable evening even if the transmission system didn't work as interestingly or effectively as one might have anticipated.

Linkages with local celebrities and habitants of West Berlin were not made informally. The way it worked was this: if there was someone in particular that you wished to meet, this person was invited with you to one of the regular cocktail parties at the British Centre. You would be formally introduced by either Captain Baker, the officer in charge, or one of his subordinates and then arrangements would be made to either visit with him or her or for them to visit you at a later stage. Indeed, my visit to the van de Graaf Laboratory of the Frei Universität was made through one of these contacts, initiated I must say, in this case, by the British Centre. But the personal contact took place over a couple of white ladies, these being drinks of course, at a cocktail party. That this system was vulnerable came first to my attention when, after being introduced to various people at such an encounter, I found myself chatting with a Dr Krayhaan from Humboldt University which is in East Berlin, and if I remember rightly near the Unter den Linden. Dr Krayhaan invited me to go on a tour of that university and to meet with several of his classes. Thinking that this had been set up by the British Centre, I accepted with some alacrity. It was only after my arranging to meet with Dr Krayhaan at Friedrichstrasse subway station on the following morning that Baker came to me and said, 'You know you're on your own. This has not been arranged by the British Centre and, whereas we have no reason to believe that you will come to any harm, it's entirely in your own hands and the British Centre is not responsible for your protection.' However, it had been arranged that all the youth leaders were to visit the West Berlin Opera on the evening of that day, so it was made clear to Krayhaan that I was required to be back safely in the British sector by six o'clock. Everything went according to plan, at least in the early stages. I was duly met, visited the university, and was taken into several classes, and introduced in German at some length. Then, on at least one occasion, I was asked to tell them if the students really look malnourished, inferior to Western students, less alert, or any of these things. Of course, I was able to say they looked like students anywhere in the world, except that I did feel that they were perhaps more attentive to everything that was said than in some of the classes that I had both participated in and recently given. After leaving the university, my host took me to his home for tea, which was situated some distance from the city, and I believe in East Germany. He wished me to stay for dinner and discuss academic matters, and it became clear that my immediate return to West Berlin was in no sense a priority to him. By late afternoon no action in relation to my return to the British sector was in place so I was eventually forced to indicate that I would be leaving whether he would take me or not and I requested that he put me in touch by telephone directly with the British Centre. There was much procrastination and prevarication before I was belatedly escorted to his car and finally dropped off at the boundary between East and West Berlin. It is true that nothing untoward happened. It is also true that I felt particularly vulnerable, and knowing that the people who had brought you to Berlin would not be responsible in any way for your health or safety while away from the British sector did little to relax the spirits of the wanderer. However, a spirited production of *Il Seraglio*, the Mozart opera, by the West Berlin Opera Company, enabled the restoration of my equanimity later that evening.

The visit to Humboldt University was not the only excursion taken by me as an individual to the eastern sector. I was particularly interested in a film called *Du und München Kamarad* which was being shown to the public indicating the events of the holocaust and what Germans had done to the Jews during wartime. I went to see it because the film was widely publicised in the eastern sector and it was regarded as almost obligatory for disciplinary and cultural reasons for citizens of that part of Berlin to be aware of the horrors that had been caused by members of the German public during the war. The cinema itself was full to overflowing and it didn't take long to find that there were no punches being pulled in this film which was as horrific as one might imagine. When some short while into the film several people near to me stood up and attempted to leave, they were forcibly restrained from doing so with cries from police inside the cinema of '*Zitzen sie*'. Back they went and we all sat there as a captive audience until the last credits were rolled.

On another occasion I walked from the western to the eastern sector and was surprised to discover, as I examined the ruins of the Reichstag and was about to return to base, that I had forgotten to bring my passport with me. Now this was a hanging offence if ever there was one, and a mistake that I have not made previously nor did after that time. I found myself being approached by an East German policeman as I approached the demarcation line between the eastern and western sectors. The policeman spoke to me in German and I shook my head indicating that I didn't speak German and was a tourist. He shook his head somewhat dramatically, threw up his hands, and walked away. Fortunately, he did not ask me for my passport. I was much more careful after that occasion.

Back in West Berlin, regular trips to the Kufurstendam and some of the major stores on that street like the KaDeWe featured in our leisure hours. Shops with cuckoo clocks and other artefacts seemed to be ubiquitous in Germany. One of the more dramatic afternoons spent in West Berlin took place when I went on a sailing trip with some students from the Free University on that great inland lake in the city called the Wansee. We had barely sailed away from the dock when once again, as in Greece, a great storm came up that bent the trees in the Tiergarten almost horizontal. We immediately dropped anchor, hauled down the sails, and sat down below in a circle of five people, drank schnapps and had a mutually unintelligible conversation for something like three hours while the yacht pitched at its point of anchorage. The little German inns around the lake and by the dock seemed particularly attractive when you were pitching up and down in the depths of the Wansee. It was certainly a relief when the wind eventually dropped somewhat and we could limp back to our point of origin.

The trip to West Berlin finally ended when we returned to Hanover by military train from Berlin, the same way by which we had arrived. It was with a mixture of relief and a sense of accomplishment that we finally left the train. Travelling in a train with all its blinds down, bound from Berlin to West Germany proper, was itself a rather eerie experience and it was with satisfaction that we finally rolled into Hanover station and started the final phase of our return to Britain and, in my case, for almost the last time to Belfast. The several exigencies and extravagances of my trip to West Berlin were the subject of articles in the *Belfast Newsletter* on my return, and helped me to reinforce my memory with topical writings that might be recovered at another time.

I was now of course a doctor of philosophy and about to leave for distant fields if not necessarily greener pastures. The writing experience and associated observational skills acquired on my travels were essentially beneficial to the career of the theoretical physicist.

Chapter Six
The Physicist at Play

From the earliest days at high school, the philosophy of a healthy mind in a healthy body was propounded with enthusiasm. Every student was not only encouraged but expected to participate in at least two sports on regular occasions, and academic and athletic success were felt in some sense to be related, although the basis for that hypothesis was not clear. As a student in my final two years at Campbell College, I participated vigorously and semi-competitively in rugby, tennis and field hockey. My enthusiasm for rugby was to some extent modified by my poor eyesight without glasses, and as contact lenses did not exist in the late Forties, running with the ball was much easier than finding it. However, rugby was a sport I followed with enthusiasm and indeed still do.

Field hockey was, on the other hand, an activity in which a bespectacled student and later physicist could participate on a level playing field, so to speak, and I did so with vigour and only a little skill. It was also a sport that I later played for many years in England until the Pickwick Festival in Birmingham in 1963. In a vital match against Bournville, I was having a better than usual game at right full-back, and frustrating the opposing inside forward to an obvious degree. Eventually, early in the second half of the game, when I had taken the ball from this character for the umpteenth time, he swung his stick in anger, broke the armoured lens of my right eyeglass, which then penetrated my eye proper and ruptured the lens. I remember vividly the slow clouding of the eye as the surrounding humour entered the lens, and I knew instinctively that that was that. When you have two working eyes, the loss of one may not seem a disaster. However, when you have only one left, prudent care of the survivor is of the essence. So ended my hockey career.

Field hockey is however an interesting game, and one which can be a delight to play but less than exciting to watch. At Campbell College, where I captained the first XI (1947–1948), largely I think because my godfather Kenneth Armour was in charge, the playing field was flat, even and kept in immaculate condition. Elsewhere in Northern Ireland, the situation was totally different. I recall playing for Queen's University against Raphoe in County Donegal in the Irish Junior Cup, and having to chase sheep off the field before play could start. There were also grounds so uneven that the top of one corner flag could not be seen from the other diagonally opposite. Grounds sloping uphill from both ends were not uncommon, and important league matches were often played in appalling conditions. Injuries were frequent, and many players took their lives in their hands when playing rural teams such as Parkview and Mossley. On one occasion when playing for Queen's University against Portrush, away, an incident occurred which was not untypical for a league match. The field was situated by the two-mile beach to the White Rocks, and covered in light sand and a few rabbit holes of recent vintage. In taking a free hit early in the game, I managed to undercut the shot, and hit a large and imposing Portrush forward right between the eyes. He went down like a poled ox and was transported to Coleraine Cottage Hospital. I thought I must have killed him, but the game continued, and finally we lost 2–1. When the match ended, half the

Portrush team descended on me, and my colleagues assumed that retribution was at hand. However, their captain extended his hand and told me not to give the violent incident another thought. As he said 'Willie is a wee bit weak in the head and that sort of thing is always happening to him!' While I must say I was relieved I am not really sure that Willie got the sympathy and comfort he deserved. Clearly, field hockey can be detrimental to your health.

In the late 1940s, coaching of sports began to play a major role in successful athletic performance. At Campbell College this would-be physicist was encouraged to combine A level examination studies with a winter tennis course for promising students. As a result, I spent two nights a week beating a tennis ball against a wall under the eagle eye of coach, Walter Lytle. The training ended with match play on a wooden indoor court, very fast and quite demanding. Having completed this course I could not wait to get out on to a real tennis court and put my new skills into practice. What I learnt was that tennis is a microcosm of life, with all the deviousness, cheating, and deceit of the real world writ large.

I had joined the Church of Ireland Young Men's Society Tennis Club at Belmont, and entered for the Open Singles Championship. My first round match was to be played against a middle-aged fellow, who I then did not know, called Norman Palmer, or 'first round Palmer' as he was designated on the amateur tennis circuit in Northern Ireland. His singular lack of success was known to everyone but me. He called me up at home to ask if we might play in the late afternoon because he would be away in the evening of the appointed day on business. The only problem left, if I was agreeable to the change, was that no umpires would be available. However, he felt that two honest and respectable people like ourselves would have no difficulty with that, and I agreed.

When I arrived at the clubhouse, Norman Palmer was already on court serving innumerable tennis balls seriatim, wearing a large towel around his neck and trying to decide between his five tennis rackets which would be best for this occasion. I had only one racket and no towel. I assumed balls would be provided and all I had to do was play. I knew at once that this would be a short encounter despite my coaching and technique. Something was very badly wrong.

In essence I was beaten by gamesmanship and craft. I had my newly learnt rules of play which turned out to be unreliable in a real world situation. Firstly, the warm-up! 'Take as long as you like,' said he, and I played according to my coach's instructions. My serve was fairly powerful, and it should not have been a problem. The warm-up period would enable me to establish Palmer's weaknesses. Was his backhand weak? If so, play several shots wide to forehand and then switch the shot, in real play, so that the vital stroke went to his area of weakness. Try a lob and see if he can deal with it. If not, store the information away and await your opportunity to take advantage later. Well, the knock-up went according to plan I thought. His forehand appeared quite reliable and he was concentrating visibly on his stroke. However, any time I switched to his backhand he was clearly in trouble, either missing the shot, or holding up his hand and shouting 'Too good for me!' He also completely fluffed my only lob.

Now the real match began. It lasted for twenty-five minutes and I lost 6–2, 6–1. Eventually I was so demoralised that I served three double faults in a row. One game in which I led 40–30 and he hit out was brought back to deuce because I caught the ball five metres beyond the baseline. Norman Palmer was able to direct me to the precise page and article in the Lawn Tennis Association Handbook where this action is forbidden and the point forfeited to the opponent.

Only some weeks later did I discover the enormity of my defeat. The wily old codger knew all about coaching and knock-ups and how to defeat them. The strongest part of his game, as everyone in the world seemed to know, was his backhand, not his forehand. In fact he possessed a fine topspin cross court backhand but a very weak all-round game. He could also smash when the occasion arose. During the knock-ups he was in fact not practising his tennis skills at all. He was doing everything to demonstrate his forehand shots, and give the additional impression of a non-existent backhand game – and I fell for it. The longer the game continued, the more I played to his strengths. Having made my initial diagnosis, it never occurred to me to revise my assumptions. What an idiot I was shown to be!

The defeat however was salutary. I did not know that all first-round losers were automatically entered in the Gentlemen's Plate Competition. This was an unexpected chance to redeem myself, and so I did, reaching the final after two weeks of matches. The final itself was almost over before it started. My opponent, a young and gifted stroke-player, Roger Lowry, was a much better tennis player than me, and clearly playing good tennis would not be the way to beat him. For nine games I matched him virtually stroke for stroke, except that he kept winning the games. By the time he was up by six games to love and four games to one, desperation was at hand. However my recent conqueror, Norman Palmer, was watching and as I walked to the back of the court to pick up a ball, he whispered to me, 'Forget about all your strokes and training, play a few nasty little drop shots and mix in a lob or two from the baseline. Slow the game up and he will fall apart'. And so he did. He won only one more game. In fact, he fell twice, running for drop shots, which didn't help either his appearance or his temper. He mishit innumerable lobs and finished the match with four double faults.

Since then, my tennis has been far from beautiful, but I have had great exercise and some success. The experience taught me much about the real world, about what can be accomplished and how to surprise even yourself from time to time. Educated pragmatism in tennis and physics should never be underrated or undervalued. Physics is, after all, not only the 'science of the probable' but, like politics, the 'art of the possible'.

In other fields of sporting endeavour my patience and concentration were often found wanting. Cricket in particular I found boring, even when my personal performance was better than usual. On the occasion of the annual staff cricket match at Birmingham in summer 1970, my great friend and crystallographer, Tom Lomer, and I batted from lunch to tea, and then afterwards, without scoring more than a handful of runs between us. To be so boring on a glorious summer afternoon scarcely added to the overall entertainment. On another occasion, playing in an evening match, the home side (mine) had declared at some huge score without the necessity of my having to bat. Late in the game I was standing with arms folded in the outfield, square of the wicket, and, I now believe, essentially asleep. A lofted square cut from the batsman at the crease failed to reach the boundary only because I was in the way. Instinctively I somehow clasped my hands around the ball, and became an instant hero. It took at least four weeks for the team to rediscover the fact that I was not a cricketer.

Many physicists however were keen and competent players. But even the best can be distracted at some point during a long afternoon or evening's cricket. Herbie Martin, who was not only a good physicist but also played cricket for Ireland as mentioned earlier, was of course a star of the Queen's University Staff cricket team. I, when appointed a faculty member at Queen's, often subbed or just supported the games. Now Martin was an excellent slip fielder, and would never normally drop a catch in any class of cricket. However, the staff wicketkeeper in the early Fifties was a law lecturer with the nickname of Windy. The reason for this appellation was clear if you were present at a match in which he played. Every time a faster ball from one of his bowlers kept low, the wicket keeper, a man of considerable girth, would crouch down to take the ball with great rapidity and break wind with reverberations seldom equalled and never surpassed. Martin, I fear, missed several slip catches in one game due entirely to Windy's efforts. By the time that the ball had reached the batsman and been diverted to the slip fielder, Martin was lying on his back helpless with laughter and in hysterical misbelief. Memories, however, are made of this.

Chapter Seven

The Physicist as a Thespian

This physicist's acting career, if such it might be called, really began at Campbell College at the age of seventeen. With no previous experience or interest in treading the boards, I was offered the minimal role of old man in Shakespeare's *Macbeth*, the annual school play. At the first rehearsal my part was exchanged for that of Ross, scarcely a major change. Two weeks later however I was further upgraded to play the part of Banquo, a character that I was more than happy to take, and apparently competent in doing so. Then, one week prior to production, the unthinkable happened, Macbeth developed scarlet fever. With seven days to prepare, learn lines, and rehearse, I was suddenly Macbeth.

Now the reason for my being offered the title role was simple. Every second week in English class, students were required to learn a new poem and be prepared to recite it on Monday in class. Most students selected a short sonnet or ode for the job, but I was known to choose lengthy narrative poems such as *Edinburgh after Flodden* or *Michael* or even *The Ancient Mariner*. I was usually word perfect and used to delight in the task. At that stage in life I had an almost perfect photographic memory, but that did not mean that I could act! And so, the opening night arrived and I knew by now almost every word of the play. As scenes are often rehearsed in random order it took a fair amount of production management to ensure that Macbeth knew which scene he was performing. All went well. Scenes with the new Banquo were the most difficult as I was mouthing all his lines for him, but nonetheless the effort, if not the acting on my part, was creditable and the school was visibly relieved.

On entering Queen's University to study physics, I was uncertain as to whether the Dramatic Society would complement or annihilate my science, but I decided to give the acting a whirl. As Claudio in *Measure for Measure*, I learnt to act a little. Larry Lerner, the producer, was inordinately patient, and the play was a considerable success, due to the acting talents of the principals Joan Moore and Denys Hawthorne. My family was not sure whether I should be crawling over a major stage on hands and knees beseeching my 'sister' to give up her virginity so that I might live. Nonetheless, I found the process of communication through dramatic prose and poetry a fascinating one. I believe my university experience broadened and enlightened me more than I could have expected.

The following year saw the Dramatic Society deeply immersed in the immortal bard's *Hamlet*. I was cast as Horatio. All went well until my first rehearsal with the key actor in the piece. Hamlet was a graduate from RADA (the Royal Academy of Dramatic Art). He was of medium height, had a great stage presence and moved really well. He was also quite a few inches shorter than Horatio, and it did not take long for the production crew to determine that I did not look appropriate for my part in the play. And so my major days as a thespian were almost over, but not quite. My later role, while a graduate student, as a sex-starved Roman in *Lysistrata* by Aristophanes got a mention in Vice-Chancellor Sir Eric Ashby's annual report. I believe it was the fact that I was president of the Students Representative Council at the time that warranted such attention. And finally on this topic, my performance as an old man in the play *Thompson in Tir-na-Nog* won me an honourable mention at the National Drama Festival in Dublin. It was clearly time to retire from the stage, and to use such dramatic talents as I possessed in communicating physical science to students, physicists and anyone else who might be prepared to listen.

Chapter Eight
The Physicist at Birmingham University

Upon my graduation as a doctor of philosophy – the overly grand title that does little to identify the skills, if any, of the holder – the job market was undoubtedly good. Local grammar schools were offering many attractive incentives to potential and promising new scientists and I distinctly recall the headmaster of Portora Royal School making approximately monthly visits from Enniskillen to Belfast in order to enlist my services as head of science. But other opportunities lay abroad. I had earlier been wooed extravagantly by a Brigadier Broadhurst, one of Glub Pasha's men, as a potential lecturer in physics to the Arab Legion. A letter to King Abdullah in introduction had already been written in 1952, and the advantages of a £2000 a year tax-free starting salary with batman and cook provided seemed almost too good to be true. Even five years would have set me up for life. However, the brigadier had warned, those weekends in Jerusalem can certainly take their toll in funds and energy. I was never to experience such delights, succumbing instead to the lure of £500 a year taxable as a full lecturer at the University of Birmingham in the Midlands of England.

The early to mid-Sixties were of course a time of great expansion in both the number of universities and of academic staff. Being already a tried rather than tired assistant lecturer I was prepared to apply for any academic position judged suitable by my supervisor, now in Glasgow, and other faculty members in the Department of Physics, who knew in detail what each institution had to offer from the career point of view.

It so happened that among several new appointments advertised in the spring of 1956, two were particularly attractive. One was for a position at Birmingham University in England in an expanding department which was completing construction of the highest energy particle accelerator to have been designed in the world at that time. The second was at Hull University in Yorkshire, a smaller department in a much smaller city but one with a high reputation in X-ray and condensed matter physics.

The trip to Birmingham for interview was uneventful. I was impressed by the greenness of the city and the beauty of the university buildings which were built around a glorious campanile placed in the centre of a semicircle of copper domed structures including a majestic great hall with a fine organ and galleries. The large playing field below, which was already much too small for the demands placed upon it, completed a multi-level elevation of character known to most people in Birmingham, if not in England, for its uncharacteristic red brick charm. Interview day comprised a tour of laboratories and lecture theatres and the interview itself.

Professor Ibbs, who was then standing down as department head, was chair of the committee, exuding benevolence and warmth, and making each candidate feel they would be welcome at the university should they be successful, and honoured to have been selected for interview, if not.

On hearing that my application to the Department of Physics at Birmingham had been successful, I withdrew from interview at Hull and planned for a future career in the Midlands of England.

That career would see me progress to the position of Senior Lecturer in 1964, and eventually to a further career in Manitoba after eighteen years of challenge and change in Birmingham.

The dominating characteristic of Birmingham as a city is the language of its people. 'Brummies' as they are called after Brummagem, the ancient name of the city, speak a dialect that is virtually unintelligible even to English from other parts of Albion.

The day of my arrival in Birmingham was one on which I had not unusually left my shaving kit on the ship by which I had travelled from Belfast to Liverpool. I therefore went shopping in Selly Oak with a view to replacing my shaving kit and on presenting payment was asked, 'Do ye moind yer choinge in threepinny beets?' Being totally unable to respond to this request after two repetitions, the chemist himself came out and translated for me. 'She wants to know if you would mind if your change was all in threepenny pieces, as we are momentarily short of cash.' Well, of course there was no problem, but a new language in which 'i' was pronounced 'ee' or occasionally 'oi' took more than a week or two to master. After a casual meeting, or even after an evening in the pub, friends would part, not with goodbyes, but with the incredible farewell 'tarar a beet' meaning 'goodbye for a little while'. This culture shock was certainly unexpected.

A colleague of mine, Brian Lowry, from the executive of the Students Representative Council at Belfast, came to a resident clinician's position at the Queen Elizabeth Hospital close by the university shortly after my arrival in Birmingham. On his first night in emergency, a young woman was brought to him, and in his best bedside manner he asked her what appeared to be the problem. 'Eats me oi doctor, eet urts.' Again, Brian, unable to decipher the code himself, was forced to call in an interpreter who translated her message into the much more helpful 'It's my eye doctor, it hurts'. As in all the best true tales this story had a happy ending and Dr Lowry, in his accustomed way, did his stuff. The eye was saved.

My first lodgings in Birmingham were in a rooming house run by a Mrs Peacock on Selly Park Road. She accommodated about eight guests for the sum of £3.10 per person per week. The area was an old and charming part of south Birmingham, and the walk to the university took only about ten minutes.

During my university career in Belfast, one of the most respected of modern poets was the Northern Irish-born Louis MacNeice, for some time a lecturer at Birmingham University. He was notable for the fact that he was undoubtedly the worst reader of his own poetry imaginable. Having heard him reading his own work in public, I can personally attest to the fact. I had been interested in poetry since my school days when I rose to the dizzy heights of runner-up for the John Bartley Verse Prize at Campbell College, I had read all of Louis MacNeice and T.S. Eliot while at university, and I knew many of their verses by heart. One poem of MacNeice's in particular, entitled *Ode*, had started, 'The night is coarse with chocolate, the wind blowing from Bournville, and I hanker for the Atlantic with a frivolous nostalgia.' Now, I had never imagined that Bournville was a part of Birmingham city. In fact Bournville Garden Village with its carillon and school, where my children, incidentally, would later learn to enjoy academic things together with its famous chocolate factory, made it one of the most attractive and popular residential areas near the university.

So, one evening in November, about two weeks after taking up my appointment, I was walking home on a muggy damp evening when suddenly the night became truly 'coarse with chocolate'. When I got to Mrs Peacock's I was able to rub my face with a finger and then taste the chocolate on it. From that experience I deduced that Bournville must be nearby, and of course that MacNeice had pioneered the academic path from Belfast to Birmingham that I was following.

My lodgings in Selly Park were adequate for a time, but having to go elsewhere for most meals except on Sundays, and the lack of anywhere to go apart from my smallish bed-sitting room made me decide to look for more attractive and flexible accommodation. My transition to the world of freedom and independence was accomplished thanks to the good offices of Andrew Le Blanc Smith, with no hyphens. Andrew was a long-time member of the field hockey club that I had recently joined at Edgbaston in Birmingham.

Edgbaston Hockey Club was by any English standards fairly snooty. Cravats and chokers abounded, and much communication between members occurred through jargon that a poor Irish lecturer had difficulty in deciphering.

Anyway, one Saturday evening, round the bar after a match, I mentioned my intention to get out of Mrs Peacock's clutches as soon as possible and to look for a suitable apartment. Well, it transpired that a ground floor apartment shared by two of my fellow players was entering uncertain times because one of them had been transferred out of town and an immediate and suitable replacement was required. After several beers I became identified as the man most likely to join Le Blanc Smith in his castle. The move was accomplished some two weeks later, though whether Mrs Peacock cared or not was hard to say. She had two daughters either on or behind the stage, and spent most of her efforts in keeping the young Peacock residents and the strutting peacock-like guests apart.

Life with Andrew LBS was not exactly a bundle of laughs. I should have known that would be the case when he told me never to hyphenate his surname as only lower classes of the gentry ever did that. While having a basically pleasant if dull demeanour, Andrew turned out to be such a stickler for timing and order that this Irishman often was tempted to hoist him with a small petard, just for the privilege of a little peace and disorder. When at home he tidied incessantly. When I left for work later than he did I would on principle leave the morning paper lying unfolded and awry somewhere off centre on the lounge coffee table, just for the fun of tracking it down late in the evening when it would be stacked in its rightful place, carefully folded and directly above the equivalent version of the previous day. Breakfast chores were alternated according to a master list prepared by ALBS, as was the cleaning excitement. To bring a friend, enemy or stray person home required a degree of planning and arrangement of Churchillian proportions. To cut a long story short, I broke up this 'happy' relationship in short order, paid my month in advance, and finally arrived at Shangri-La, on Stirling Road near the Ivy Bush where I was at last king of a considerable, if grotty, first floor kingdom that was nothing but mine own as long as I paid the rent, a princely five pounds per week.

Despite moving west of my original abode, I continued to play intermittently for Edgbaston Club, mostly for the second XI but occasionally when the Club was in desperate straits for their first XI.

There was one memorable occasion when playing at home, a large bull escaped from the local slaughter yards and succeeded in eluding police, veterinarians and the public, only to arrive in the vicinity of Edgbaston Park Road in time for the bully off in our Saturday match. The side as a whole plus supporters exhibited little bravery on that occasion.

Anyway, it transpired that my old friend and colleague, Brian Lowry, of medical fame, was enlisted also in the ranks of Edgbaston Hockey Club. He was quite an asset, being currently an Irish International full-back. Now I, being a poverty stricken academic had relinquished my wheels when I left the family car back in Belfast, and depended upon shank's mare and the all-night bus service to carry me from A to B, and back if necessary. Brian, on the other hand, had purchased a rather nifty motorcycle, probably a local Norton, and occasionally when he and I were playing on the same team we would ride together on the bike, parking it carefully among the Rovers, Jaguars and Aston Martins of our very respectable English colleagues.

Nonetheless, despite the fact that most club members had no transportation problems, occasionally a new member, or one with unforeseen technical problems would seek a ride on Brian's bike. If the need was identified then Brian would receive with his weekly game card saying, for example, 'You have been selected to play for Edgbaston first XI on Saturday 11th March, 1958, against Womborne away', a note of unintelligible import, saying for example, 'Bring P.T.'. Brian would have no idea who or what P.T. was but usually P.T. would turn out to be someone identifiable by such initials, say Peter Trump, who would call up on Friday evening and arrange for a lift to the game. In principle the scheme was simple enough.

But as spring approached and the season ended, an additional card came reminding all members of the Club Annual Dinner and Ball at the Clubhouse at 8 p.m. On this occasion Brian's card had the cryptic codicil: 'bring D.J.'. Well, Brian did not know who D.J. was, and as he didn't call, both Brian and I headed off in our best cotton socks and ties to the gala evening – pay at the door. On arrival, a very spiffily dressed ALBS and someone else met us at the door in horrified confusion.

'Did you not read the note on the card?' the secretary of the Club asked.

'I did,' said Brian, 'but he didn't call.'

'You were supposed to bring a dinner jacket,' said our fellow team member. 'I am sorry but we can't let you in.'

Well, talk about flummoxed. Brian and I thought of interesting things to do such as taking the clubhouse apart. However, having been educated at Queen's University where dinner jackets and indeed tails were common attire for all aspiring undergraduates, quite apart from graduate students, and where there was on average a formal ball a week throughout the academic year, we decided to show them who it was had class. Eventually, halfway through the dinner two sartorial, if no longer sober, Irishmen took their places at an always to be forgotten event notable more for its pomposity than team spirit.

Shortly thereafter, Brian and I went our different ways, both destined to finally pitch our tents on the eternal Canadian prairies. In the interim I happily transferred my enthusiasm and limited skills in field hockey to Kings Heath Hockey Club where I met more friends and had more hilarious enjoyment than at any time before or since in my time on the athletic scene.

My lecturing chores at Birmingham University were nothing if not varied and challenging. On arrival I found myself assigned to a course of lectures to pre-medical and pre-dental students from all over the world taking physics as a compulsory prerequisite. 1956, of course, was the year of the Hungarian revolution, and many students arrived in Britain as refugees towards the end of the year. I recall one morning seeing a new clean and eager face in the front row of my lecture, following every word I said and nodding appreciatively at every point which I clarified or emphasised for the class. When class had finished I was not surprised to find this student standing in line with those asking further questions, and eventually when his turn came he said clearly enough, 'Excuse me, but I speak not the English.' I remember feeling totally deflated, for in fact I had addressed the whole lecture to him directly, gauging its import and effectiveness through the mirror of his facial expression.

In contrast to the elementary teaching, I shared responsibility for the final-year quantum mechanics class with Paul T. Matthews, later to become Chair of Physics at Imperial College and tragically killed in a bicycle accident in Cambridge in 1989.

I gave a series of one hour problem classes while Paul gave the lectures, very much in the style of his book published several years later. Although we met regularly, occasionally with (now Sir) Sam Edwards to ensure that our courses were complementing each other, the final examination was set entirely by Paul with the good housekeeping seal of approval from the external examiner for the Physics degree course. I merely attempted to prepare the students for this problem-oriented paper and to give them the confidence to tackle anything the examiners might hurl at them. In fact, the students were so uniformly successful in this examination that a class average of eighty per cent or so was recorded, much to the embarrassment of the department which could not believe that the paper was an adequate test of students' ability. Matthews assured the head, P.B. Moon, and the external examiner that anyone who obtained a high mark on this paper was worthy of his or her mark and that perhaps at last, here was a class with fairly uniform abilities in mathematical physics. Despite great scepticism from the rest of the department, the marks were allowed to stand. Many years after, I recall Paul chuckling over the success of this tandem-teaching model for undergraduate quantum mechanics.

Lecturing in some of the theatres in the physics department was not always easy. In the late Fifties, a new Nuffield building was opened with new staff offices and a lecture theatre to cater to approximately a hundred students. It became the site for colloquia, special evening lectures, freshmen's day addresses and so forth. It was also the venue for many of the second- and third-year physics classes. As a forward looking gesture, each staff office was equipped with a variable air intake valve which effectively conditioned the office. The lecture theatre, however, while possessing a larger and similar air conditioning system, had no manual adjustment of flow. This might not have been a problem had air pressure been regulated in some way, but unfortunately a constant volume of air per second was transported through the system, winter or summer, day or night. As a result, on a cool winter day, air intake into the staff offices was reduced to a minimum, while a powerful jet of air blew into the lecture theatre and in fact vertically downwards to the point at which I invariably placed my lecture notes. To this day the chaotic ceremony of the recovery of the lecturer's notes is still recalled with affection by former students. As someone said, 'It certainly woke everybody up when it occurred at eight thirty in the morning.'

The situation of this, the so-called New Lecture Theatre, was somewhat bizarre comprising the only direct access for maintenance purposes to the first floor roof area and air conditioning facilities. Early in the existence of the new facility a contract was completed with a construction firm to erect a kind of pump room on this small roof area, and buckets of cement would be regularly transported by hand from inside the building to the roof via the lecture theatre, even while lectures were proceeding. For some reason, however, it was always my 10.30 to 11.30 lecture spot that was cement delivery time, and I really did not know how to deal with it.

For example, I would be writing on the blackboard when a small hairy and unkempt leprechaun of a man would enter backside first from the door beside me, waddle painfully up the inclined steps to the back door and then crash blindingly into the sunshine beyond, spilling cement continuously as he went, but saying nothing – not an excuse me, sorry, or by your leave. Ten minutes later the process would be reversed and the purveyor of cement would return his bucket or buckets by the reverse route. I went along with this for two lectures but by then the class was no longer listening to me at all. They were awaiting the cement delivery with an anticipation that bordered on fascination. So when the little man appeared for the third time in one hour, behind first, through the door to the now unconcealed delight of the students, I laid down my chalk, strode into the stairway between lecture seats, held up my hands and said, 'Stop this. I am sorry but you can't interrupt a lecture in this way.' At this time he dropped both buckets to the floor simultaneously, pulled himself up to his gargantuan five feet six inches, looked me straight in the eye and said very loudly: 'And how else do you suggest my mates might get their cement?' Having spoken, he then, like a weightlifter about to perform some heroic feat, again raised his buckets into the air and slopped his way to the back of the room, crashing even more noisily on to the roof than before. Unable to deal with this rather public situation, I took my concerns to the head of the department. He, I suspect, had no more success than I in addressing the problem and the contract involved.

Thankfully, one week later the contract was completed, and physics again held sway over abnormal deliveries of the Portland product.

Perhaps the most challenging of assignments allocated to me during my time at Birmingham was the organisation and delivery of physics instruction to what were called subsidiary physics students. These would be majoring, if we can use that word in the English context, in some subject other than physics, including production engineering, geography, mathematics, chemistry, biology, and a variety of others, up to a dozen in all. The lectures took place in the old Poynting Lecture Theatre which accommodated up to three hundred souls, with the students sitting in tiered splendour in rows that disappeared into the back of the room and final invisibility.

The lecturer prior to me had retired somewhat prematurely as a result of continued harassment from this class of non-physicists. Stories were told of the hundred pigeons released in his final lecture, somewhere from the depths of the theatre, and his exit in flight at an early stage in his delivery. On another occasion a boulder of considerable size was rolled from top to bottom of the aisle midway through a lecture, crashing with a fearful splintering of wood into the huge lecture and demonstration table in front. The entry of a half-naked woman into a class while in progress, on the other hand, while entertaining for the students, was apparently unobserved by the teacher. He had already become so distraught by his teaching assignment that he made a point of never looking in the direction of the class.

Anyway, my task was to interest this unlikely mob in physics, for not only were they traditionally unruly and inattentive, they were failing the course in droves and pressure from other departments was building for them to teach the physics required in their own departments. The problem of enlisting the support of these students in the teaching itself seemed important to me, so my first initiative was to set up a staff/student committee representative of each of the subgroups on the subsidiary physics course, and meet with them on a regular basis. The committee, comprising some eight students and myself, discussed the methods of teaching and their effectiveness, the incorporation of more applied projects in the laboratory, the uniformity or otherwise of the laboratory marking scheme, and such other topics as might be appropriate at any given time. The students were elected from their individual laboratory classes by their peers, these classes being more informal and of course much smaller than the lecture throng, and they in turn elected a secretary, drew up the fortnightly agenda, and made a real success of what originally was little more than an embryonic idea.

With departmental support, I built a wind tunnel and windspeed measuring equipment which was of interest and relevance to the engineers while demonstrating fundamental facts of physics. An environmental evaluation kit which was used to measure pH of soil, humidity, temperature, thermal and electrical conductivity of leaves, and other physical qualities, enabled biologists to study small ecosystems in detail. In this way physics was made less remote a discipline for many, and the concept of thinking like a physicist was encouraged from the first lecture onward. Originally, certain parts of the course I inherited were as dull as ditchwater even to a dedicated physicist.

The lecture on photometry, which involved teaching the units of measurement of light radiation and qualitative assessment of the brightness of sources, had traditionally been drowned by the snores of the class. The student committee had learned from some student predecessors that this part of the course was likely to be a disaster, and asked if it would be possible to omit it. As part of the curriculum, of course that was not possible. However, I produced an illuminating and highly theatrical solution to the problem which succeeded beyond my wildest dreams.

As the lecture was due to start, the students were instructed by the room technician to stay in their places as the lights would be extinguished. At that moment I, as lecturer, appeared, not at the front but at the back of the theatre carrying a lighted candle, and proceeded like Lady Macbeth down the aisle to the front. The candle then became the focus of the lecture – defined as an International Standard Candle. A one metre square piece of white cardboard was brought to within one metre of the candle, and the light reflected would demonstrate an illumination of one lux. As the lecture/demonstration continued, even the most boring of all pieces of equipment, greasespot photometers, had their hour upon the stage, and although few notes were taken, much was learnt. To my great surprise, the examination question on this part of the course was one of the most popular in selection and also the best answered.

I must have improved and developed the subsidiary teaching significantly over the ten years or so in which it was one of my principal responsibilities. With Professor Moon's active encouragement and support a floating island floor was added to the laboratory in the middle Sixties, enabling a much wider variety of experiments to be assembled, and working conditions for students who were never to become physicists to be greatly improved. Technicians Bob Roberts and Len Harwood performed heroic deeds in support of my sometimes unorthodox ideas. Pank Stait also gave invaluable assistance with design of equipment for which no prototype was available. All in all, both the students and I learned a lot in those days and my discovery of the value of applied physics projects in the teaching of physics itself was to prove invaluable to me later on, particularly in Manitoba, Canada.

Philip Burton Moon, Head of the Department and later Dean of the Faculty of Science and Engineering, was undoubtedly the best physicist at Birmingham University.

He had imagination, vision and a deep understanding of physics and its relationship to technical things. He was also a stickler for precision in both the spoken and written word.

I recall vividly the only occasion on which I was hauled over the coals by Professor Moon. The incident occurred about two years after my assumption of the position of lecturer and somewhat after the end of my probationary period. Examination time was approaching and each examiner was required to provide a completed question paper, including one or two additional questions in case either Philip Moon or the external examiner for the department, a physicist at Bristol I believe at the time, thought one of the questions submitted inappropriate. The role of the external examiner was to ensure the maintenance of academic standards both within and between universities, and the task as performed at Birmingham was a highly onerous one.

Well, for a first-year physics course which I was giving at the time, I compiled a collection of classical mechanics, electricity and magnetism questions, the latter embracing elementary optics. Having invented a series of original questions of my own I selected two from a much earlier Cambridge Tripos examination and included them verbatim in the question paper. There are, after all, not a vast number of kinds of questions possible for solution in a typical first-year paper. The second of the questions selected was the one to cause the problem; it read, 'Calculate the magnification of a simple lens given that the distance of the image of an object placed x cm in front of the lens is y cm behind it.' Now, of course, as everyone knows magnification is produced by a lens and the size and position of an image depends in each case on the size and position of the object. The idea that any physicist in his or her right mind should think so sloppily as to believe that the phrase 'produced by' could be omitted implied that he or she required a very severe talking to, otherwise the whole teaching regime at Birmingham could collapse. In my defence I knew that those questions which I prepared from scratch were by and large unexceptionable in either logic or style. However, the two standard questions already accepted and used by Cambridge University in grading its students, and selected by me for use at Birmingham were both suspect, and the one mentioned in detail unacceptable. Perhaps the moral of the story was that a teacher should always generate original questions, a task of considerable difficulty and tedium. Perhaps Professor Moon felt at the time that I was developing a social life that could interfere with the normal twenty-four hours per day devotion to physics that was expected of young faculty members. Whatever the case, I felt totally deflated, terrified of ever setting a further examination, and doubtful of a genuine future in my chosen career.

I trotted out this monologue on the destruction of my self-worth to Martin Johnson, the reader in astrophysics at Birmingham University and asked him for his advice and opinion. He wisely said that it is good for physicists not to be ignored by those in authority and that I should look upon this admonition from as kind and wise a man as Philip Moon as perhaps a guide or stepping stone to greater things. Eventually I accepted his advice, and to this day I firmly believe that this simple event coming at the time it did, enabled me to redouble my efforts both in teaching and research. Indeed I believe that the same Philip Moon was instrumental in my early promotion to the rank of Senior Lecturer in physics in 1964.

Chapter Nine

The Physicist Meets Experimental Equipment and Researchers at Birmingham

The theoretical physicist was reborn in an experimental mould on appointment to the lectureship at Birmingham University. Two dramatically different research facilities available at the time were the Rotblat camera and the Birmingham synchrotron.

The Rotblat camera was a device for detecting charged particles. It was designed by Professor J. Rotblat of the Medical College of St Bartholomew's Hospital for the study of nuclear scattering and reaction processes. It consisted of a series of high density emulsion plates, the favourite detector of nuclear physicists in the Fifties, and recorded particles emitted from low energy collision processes. Gas targets were most commonly used. All tracks required individual counting under a microscope and correction for energy loss en route to the emulsion and for dip angle at the emulsion surface. The plates used were Ilford C2 products and consisted of fifty per cent or more silver bromide by weight.

Each experiment was designed with the capabilities of the camera in mind, and finding, counting and measuring tracks was a tedious, precise and soul-destroying process.

Women in general were better at such analysis than men. Indeed the patience of many faculty members and graduate students was readily exhausted by the scanning process.

Strangely enough, however, the developing need for full-time scanning personnel both for the type of work described and the fertile field of bubble chamber and wire chamber photography, brought many women into the previously male-dominated world of the physicist. Wives, sweethearts, girlfriends, and others chose to spend their days in semi-darkness searching for the elusive tracks so beloved of their employers.

On arrival at Birmingham my first task as an experimental physicist was to co-ordinate a group from London, Birmingham, Queen's Belfast and Bristol Universities whose research was based on the Rotblat camera facility, with the Birmingham Nuffield cyclotron providing the incident beams of protons, deuterons or alpha particles necessary for its use. Together with a graduate student and under the general direction of Professor Bill Burcham, I would carry out most of the experimental work. The emulsions would then be farmed out to those members of the group most involved in the design and interpretation of each experiment. The work, while being interesting in the early stages when new processes were under study, became increasingly repetitive and even uncompetitive as coincidence counting and time-of-flight measurements rose to prominence.

I rarely met Professor Rotblat although I communicated with him regularly. We did however meet at the Paris Conference of 1958 when several of the group found themselves together on a *bateau mouche* powering our way along the Seine River and under the myriad bridges that span her. Earlier it transpired that somewhere on my way through Paris to the conference I had picked up a simple pamphlet in English outlining interesting facts and features of the city. Incorporated into this broadsheet was the fascinating, but as it transpired fallacious fact that despite their differences in age and architecture all bridges over the Seine in central Paris were the same height above the river. I communicated this gem of information to Professor Rotblat as we stood chatting alone on the upper deck of the little boat, and there was no reason immediately to suspect the veracity of this piece of intelligence. It happened however that later as we were chatting amiably, face to face on deck, he with his back to the next upcoming bridge, it became clear to me that something was very wrong. At this point, whether he spun round because of the look of disbelief on my face, or whether I actually shouted 'down' I do not recall. Needless to say, we were able to reflect while lying flat on the upper deck that decapitation on a pleasure boat had almost become a reality for both of us, and that instant death would have been more than an embarrassment. In retrospect, from my point of view, this was a poor way in which to make friends and influence people in the world of physics. I have since that time been exceptionally careful never to quote from a paper not published in a properly refereed and authoritative scientific journal, or to assume that the written word in everyday publications is any real reflection of the truth. Joseph Rotblat fortunately survived to win the Nobel Peace Prize in 1995 for his work in organising and developing the Pugwash Conference series, a well-deserved reward for his initiative and example.

Since the earliest days, I have both supervised and learned from a variety of graduate students. Each has had his or her eccentricities and prejudices. Some were freethinkers always wanting to go their own way or wishing to tackle any problem other than the one in hand. Others were tentative, at least in their early years of graduate work, always preferring thought to action. Two students of a confident and assertive kind worked with me on PhD programmes in the late Sixties in Birmingham. One, Peter Dunscombe later moved to Canada becoming Head of Medical Physics at the University of Manitoba and later Head of the Cancer Foundation at Sudbury.

The other, Colin Pope, intended to become a teacher of physics in high school, but the vicissitudes of life transformed him later into a faculty member at one of the newer British universities. Working with these two budding geniuses was quite an experience in their graduate student days. Experiments involving the Radial Ridge cyclotron took several days of continuous running time to complete. The graduate students were either on night or day shift while I overlapped both. Each believed that while in charge of the experiment he could redesign, improve or rationalise the electronic time-of-flight data acquisition system in a unique and far superior way. The result was that all advances made by one during the night, were discarded once the other came on shift with his own new and improved system of operation. Trying to restore reason to this madness was a tortuous task, as everyone including the supervisor believed himself to be the ultimate arbiter of truth. Finally, after several unproductive days, compromise was reached during a brief, if confrontational, fifteen minute shift-change period, and sweetness and light returned to the few-body group and its data collection.

Colin Pope, although still a graduate student, was widely noted for his entrepreneurial activities. He preferred to work at night, largely because he would have unlimited access to computer facilities and the punch card machines for recording data. His talents it transpired did not find themselves limited to physics. He would record on cards the weekly upgraded performance of English First Division football teams, and use the sum total of performance to date, to predict the outcome of upcoming matches. His prowess at this computer-related skill became such that he invited cyclotron laboratory members, faculty and students, to invest in a 'pool' for sixpence a week. He would personally take the predictions of his, by now, highly refined programme and send off an appropriately completed football pools coupon to the sponsoring firm Littlewoods. As his supervisor, I felt obliged to encourage his computational talents, insisting only that each contributor receive a copy of his predictions each week prior to game day.

It pains me in many ways to complete this tale but let me try. Colin, as usual on this particular week had updated his programme on the basis of the previous week's results and forwarded his weekly forecast to all investors. Imagine our delight and surprise when we learned on Saturday that on the basis of the Pope forecast we had won a second dividend to the tune of around £100,000 to be divided among the six of us. Of course, until you hear officially from Littlewoods extreme euphoria would be unseemly. Perhaps a challenge to one of the home draws on which the dividend depended might be offered and sustained, unlikely as that would be. The value of the pay-out had also still to be exactly calculated. Nonetheless Monday came with an air of excitement about it like no other.

Strangely enough, Colin Pope was not to be seen. Nor was there a good news missive on computer paper awaiting our arrival at work. As time went on it became clear that all was not well, and it seems necessary to outline the tragic coda to this epic. Firstly, it was confirmed that the computer programme had indeed predicted the results that would assure a second dividend on that day. Secondly, Colin had undoubtedly sent off the coupon, in time, to Littlewoods. Thirdly, however, and more importantly he had not checked his transcription from computer programme to coupon, and had in fact incorrectly entered one home draw on the sheet. As a result, the difference in pay-out dropped from £100,000 to something like £3.10 or around fifty pence per member of the syndicate. Once the truth was revealed Colin Pope suddenly and appropriately became the least popular graduate student around. It is, to my mind, a great credit to academic integrity and the collegiality of university life that he ever graduated with a PhD degree. It is to be hoped that this excursion into the financial market served as a salutary lesson for our inefficient friend and as a warning to all of us with high financial aspirations.

It was in the summer of 1953 that the University of Birmingham synchrotron facility became the first proton synchrotron to operate at full design energy. Ten years previously Professor Markus L. Oliphant had brought forward a proposal to raise the magnetic field strength in a circular machine with particle energy in such a way that the particle orbit radius could remain fixed.[1] This design, which allowed the use of a doughnut-shaped vacuum chamber placed inside a light and comparatively inexpensive ring-shaped magnet opened the window to future advances in the energy of proton accelerators.

From a personal perspective, after joining the staff of the physics department of Birmingham University in 1956, it was some three years before I became actively involved with and worked on the synchrotron. Indeed my formative years at Birmingham, as already mentioned, were spent on the Nuffield cyclotron using the Roblat camera, attempting to work under impossible conditions with minuscule beams of alpha-particles and, later, helium-three, while all metering associated with the cyclotron oscillated wildly under the influence of the adjacent pulsed machine. There was much excitement around the university in those days. Clearly, it was a drop-in centre for any respectable physicist

---

[1] *Encyclopedia Americana*, Vol. 21, 1988, p. 493.

travelling across Europe or from the other side of the pond. Many graduate students and research assistants working in the laboratory are now in senior positions at universities and laboratories elsewhere in the Commonwealth. I think in particular of colleagues at Birmingham who are currently active as professors of physics in Canada, like David Ryan at McGill University, Bob Carnegie at Carleton and Bill Frisken at York University, all of whom are still intimately involved in particle physics at home or abroad. It is not necessary however to dwell inordinately on physics that was carried out during the lifetime of the synchrotron as that was adequately covered by review papers given at a Reunion Conference on 16th September, 1993.[2]

From my point of view, having worked with Bob Van der Raay, John Dowell and Len Riddiford at different times and on different yet somewhat related experiments, I can say that the time was one of great excitement and many challenges. Even with the development of an extracted beam facility, the difficulties in obtaining statistically significant data that would stand the test of time were significant. Some experiments such as the search for anomalous behaviour in two-pion production in the isospin-zero channel, which lasted some four months, placed significant strain on both the people involved and the equipment that was being used. I personally got great satisfaction from the first-time use of a tracking and matching program for particle transmission through magnets and lenses of various kinds. With this it was possible to calibrate and put in position all magnetic components of a 20m long scattered-proton beam line. Indeed, to find that trajectory and phase-space calculations

---

[2] Birmingham Synchroton, 40th Reunion 1993 Proceedings, Editor, P. M. Rolph. Published by University of Birmingham School of Physics and Space Research (1995).

turned out to give precisely the observed results opened up new windows of opportunity for this and future experiments.

My principal recollection of the synchrotron laboratory at this time is of the people who worked there and some of the more bizarre occurrences that took place. I recall a graduate student, Margaret Foster, in the early days bravely heading off alone to a field behind the Barber Institute to fill her polystyrene-walled target with liquid hydrogen. There was also a technician, now nameless if not blameless, who discovered a fine technique for determining whether the synchrotron beam was indeed circulating or not by looking through a quartz window in the 'doughnut', an evacuated tube circular in dimensions through which the particle beam passed, seeing light and then closing his eyes. If the light was still there when his eyes were closed the beam was circulating, otherwise not. This was an unhappy practice from which he was correctly dissuaded. More dramatic events also occurred. I recall the details of the explosion of the propane bubble chamber and the fact that Brian Musgrave, now at Argonne National Laboratory, was bending down to pick up a screwdriver at the time. This distraction certainly saved him from a much more severe injury than the cut on his head that he actually received.

I also recall that the fifteen-inch liquid hydrogen/deuterium target used in the two-pion production experiment was not infrequently in need of repair due either to a leak at the window or to cracking after recycling, that is to say repeated filling and emptying of the target. Len Riddiford, who was group leader in this particular experiment, was a man with lots of enthusiasm but not a great deal of patience and he could on occasion give vent to epithets that do not appear in the 'fair dinkum' dictionary used by all Australians. On one particular occasion when the deuterium target had burst but not exploded, Len was in somewhat of a hurry to restore the status quo and refill the target. Of course the window could not be completely removed and a new one affixed until the hydrogen in the target had been removed and the target warmed up to room temperature. I recall on one evening, when such an event had occurred, entering the laboratory to find Len warming the target up with a commutative hair dryer while the body of the reservoir sat firmly under his arm. At the same time a sheet of flame at least a metre and one-half in length was roaring from the other end of the target assembly. Apparently the sound of the hair dryer had dulled all awareness of the hydrogen blow torch that was operational just a few centimetres from the centre of his back.

This was one of several bizarre features of experimental programmes involving liquid hydrogen and deuterium targets at that time. If there was no overnight running, the liquid hydrogen target had to be observed at all times. There was a schedule of people to sleep with the target which was a somewhat eerie and unrewarding experience. There was also a research council dictum that a high-powered fan should be placed directly above any cryogenic target to minimise the danger of explosion. It became clear to all of us working in that field that the last thing you wanted to do was to mix air in with hydrogen in the event of a target rupture. The diffusion rate of hydrogen is such that nothing is normally going to stop it rising vertically in bulk, and to mix air into the path of the hydrogen more efficiently could be a recipe for disaster. Fortunately, nothing of the kind ever occurred; perhaps more by good luck than by good guidance.

The synchrotron, for some reason or other, acted as home to a number of scrawny and malnourished cats of unknown parentage. This was drawn forcibly to our attention on one occasion when data being collected during the period of four months mentioned earlier, suddenly stopped coming in and counters ceased to register the presence of any particles. Nonetheless the liquid target, the individual scintillation and Cerenkov counters all seemed to be working normally and there was a beam of about 3×10^7 protons per second emerging from the synchrotron. It was, I am sorry to say, due to the presence of one of these cats or kittens that the beam was no longer going where it should. One of them had found a collimator on a high stand to be an ideal scratching or sleeping post. It seems that for a considerable period, not less than four hours, this cat was happily altering the course of science in its own way.

While the synchrotron was operational only one member of staff was indispensable – Arthur Cleveley, the technician small enough to enter and change the brushes in the large electrical generator. Of the inebriated visitor who tottered into the laboratory one night in the late Fifties and shorted out an HT set, little can be said except that the studs on his boots became imprinted in the deck and he managed to survive the experience.

Finally, a true tale that will be told as accurately as I can recall it, for it involves a series of events that happened more than thirty years ago. A physicist from the United States, until recently a department head in an Eastern university, was on leave in England and carrying out research on the University of Birmingham Synchrotron facility. Experiments in those days took months to complete and the teams working on them developed a high degree of camaraderie, and socialised together when not actually doing research. Well, it transpired that the US visitor had a theory that he was anxious to prove, namely that you could publish anything in a popular scientific journal, fact or fiction. If you did not wish your conclusions to go through the normal refereeing process, you could write a letter to the editor, and if your name and title were authoritative and impressive enough, then publication as a letter to the editor, without review of any kind, was not only possible but guaranteed. We discussed the matter one Saturday evening over a few pints of English beer until the final scheme took form. In essence a well-known and respectable scientific journal was selected, and a letter sent describing the following phenomenon. The author, while holidaying on an island off the east coast of the United States, had suddenly found the sky grow dark, and to his surprise a significant 'rainfall' of freshwater fish took place which lasted for several minutes. Had any readers, he wondered, experienced a similar happening? The beauty of this letter lay in the fact that it described an unusual but perhaps not impossible phenomenon. The additional feature, which it was felt would guarantee publication was the identity of the author. The name itself now escapes memory, but the designation Rear Admiral US Navy retired seemed destined to guarantee success. Here was a letter from a citizen above suspicion.

Now, it should be noted that this letter to the editor was not intended to be frivolous. If published, it was intended that a follow-up letter would then reveal the complete plot and result in a tightening of refereeing standards, for this journal at least. Indeed such a letter had already been written, well in advance of a response from the publisher to the first offering. But this is where things went terribly wrong. The letter from the journal to the Rear Admiral at a holding address in the United States was not forwarded to Birmingham University, and the first notification of acceptance came in the shape of the next issue of the journal as it appeared on library shelves. There was the Rear Admiral's letter in all its glory. At this point our heroic physicist friend resolutely prepared to mail his follow-up letter in which everything is revealed. For some reason, however, a delay of several days took place, during which time a letter arrived from the publishers, this time forwarded directly from the US address. In this letter it was revealed that the Rear Admiral's observation had struck a chord of interest in the readers of the journal. Indeed two letters submitted by active scientists in their fields were to be published in an upcoming issue, each a fascinating response in itself. It is difficult now to recall precisely the nature of the two communications, but one, I believe, was from a wildlife biologist who it appeared had experienced a similar phenomenon to that described by our friend and in a similar location. The second contribution was from a geographer or climatologist who drew attention to his model for wind flow in the northern hemisphere. It described how occasionally, despite the prevailing westerly flow of air, winds can blow in precisely the opposite direction. Under such circumstances hot air from the Sahara can rise as it leaves the African continent and suck up, as in a tornado, water and fish from mountain lakes, carry them in a dust cloud for several thousand miles and then as the cloud approaches the next land mass, deposit its contents as rainfall, to the immense surprise of local people. There is little more to say. It became impossible to send the second letter without harming the careers of two practising scientists, not to mention the pseudo Rear Admiral. In the end, no further action was taken, and the whole matter became history. However, the moral of the story is clear. Without adequate refereeing procedures at all levels it is still possible to mislead even the readers of reputable scientific journals.

Chapter Ten

The Physicist Goes Courting and Plans a Honeymoon

And suddenly, there she was, Christine Savage, the gorgeous girl with the yellow hair! Golden-tanned from a family holiday in Spain, she floated effortlessly through the entrance hall of the guild of undergraduates union building at Birmingham University and directly into my consciousness. Her walk and deportment alone were an eloquent testimony to the excellence of Sheffield Girls' High School and the pride instilled in its products.

I, for my part, was idly discussing matters of concern to the university debating club and was accompanied by an eclectic group of undergraduate and graduate students, discussing future plans and programmes. Fortunately for me, one of the students saw fit to introduce me to this vision of loveliness that had just appeared and from that time on nothing in my life was ever to be the same. In that respect, it might seem strange to have a lecturer in physics chasing determinedly after a seventeen year old first-year social science student. It might even have been thought ridiculous or inappropriate. However, for some reason, perhaps because I had never left my childhood behind, or because Christine was vastly more mature than I, or indeed a mixture of both, the 'age thing' never seemed to be of any great significance and, of course, as time went on and we both got older, the age difference as a proportion of the total continued to diminish.

Nevertheless, the lifestyle of the physicist started to change somewhat dramatically. Saturday nights at the Students Union or elsewhere, became sacrosanct and major logistic hurdles were overcome in order to return the sweaty and unshaven physicist from hockey matches in darkest Worcester or Warwickshire in time for his weekly encounter with his beloved.

In the early days of our romance, Christine had lodgings with a somewhat severe woman in Haunch Lane in King's Heath. I recall vividly, on many occasions dancing hand-in-hand along this road singing songs such as *You Make Me Feel So Young* which was a favourite rendition of Old Blue Eyes and a best seller in the Midlands at that time.

There were several students staying at the house in Haunch Lane, including Christine's best friend, Erica Banks, a pretty dark-haired girl from Leeds, and the three of us used to often spend time sitting cross-legged on a table or two discussing the problems of the world and solving them without any great degree of difficulty. It was somewhat unfortunate that I was directly responsible for Christine's expulsion from this happy home.

As secretary of King's Heath hockey club, I was one of the organisers of the annual ball held at the Warwickshire County Cricket Ground and responsible for a tombola draw for which many beautiful prizes were donated by firms and organisations in the neighbourhood. On the night of the ball, I bought enough tickets for the tombola to ensure that at least one winning ticket was likely to be included and gave these to Christine as the moment of truth approached and the draw was completed. Surely enough a lucky number came up and Christine went forward to receive her prize which turned out to be less than appropriate. It was, in fact, a car sump-heater, somewhat like an Aladdin's lamp writ large. This symmetrical, if unusual object was taken home to Haunch Lane and because there was no use for it and none of our friends possessed an automobile, there it stayed for at least a few days before the landlady made her dire discovery. Finding a large, if beautiful, oil lamp with a wick in it, underneath her lodger's bed, drove her essentially ballistic. She assumed, immediately, that the warmth of the house was not regarded as adequate and that Christine had intended to light this wick and somehow or other warm the bed if cold weather continued. As a result, when Christine returned to her lodgings that particular evening, she found that she had exactly one day in which to hightail it out of Haunch Lane forever. No discussion of the matter was going to be entertained. As a result, new lodgings had to be found and immediately it transpired that, in many ways, these were to be more convenient to the bus route and to the university than was the earlier location.

The main and unique features of the new abode were that Christine's room, being on the top floor, had a small hole in the roof through which you could view stars directly without leaving the bed. The washing machine, in the kitchen area, was not available for use by tenants because it was used by the landlord to brew and store beer. There was also a young medical student staying in this house who had a habit of placing brains and other organs under study on the dinner table just as the meal was being prepared. I think her colleagues found this habit, however valuable educationally, to be somewhat distressing and disturbing to the stomach.

Nevertheless, the new lodgings were convenient to the bus and easily accessible at all hours from the university. King's Heath cricket club was situated just across the road from Christine's new abode and, in the summer, we would play tennis and occasionally watch a cricket match on the really lovely ground with its immaculate turf and pretty village green-like surroundings. One afternoon, in early summer, Christine and I found ourselves sitting at the boundary line in splendid isolation and far from such madding crowd as there was, when a singular event occurred which was later embellished around the bar by members of my hockey team who, incidentally, in the winter used the cricket club facilities. Cricket was never my favourite game and it so happened that on this Saturday afternoon, cricket was the furthest thing from my mind despite the fact that I was sitting with my beloved and watching in supposedly rapt attention. It appeared that a certain amount of cuddling was taking place between us just before the tea interval to the extent that the square leg umpire saw fit to stop the match for a moment and then proceed to march the eighty yards to the square leg boundary at great speed and with an ominous gait. It was only in the later stages of his walk that I appreciated that he was heading straight for us and assumed naively that he wanted some advice from the spectators. It transpired, however, that he felt that activities outside the field of play were detracting from the spectacle on the field and, indeed, warned us that if whatever we were doing did not cease abruptly, we would be forcibly removed from the ground. The umpire then returned to resume his position on the field of play, and some five minutes after play had stopped, it recommenced. Shortly afterwards tea was taken.

Being myself a member of King's Heath cricket club through membership of the hockey club, I was somewhat incensed at the pomposity and presumptuousness of the fellow concerned. It seemed to me at the time and still does, that a little quiet snog on a summer's afternoon might be just as appropriate an activity as gazing aimlessly at a sea of white-panted cricketers whose somnambulistic motions served only to give one a modest feeling of eternity.

Christine's father and mother lived with her brother in a house on Ridgeway Road in Sheffield. It became usual for the physicist to visit Sheffield at weekends when term was over and separation for weeks on end became inevitable. The house was pretty inside and the garden neat and fragrant so it was quite a delight to visit Sheffield in the summer and to laze around in the bosom of the family. Initially, I suspect, Mr Savage didn't know quite what to make of me, so most planning and communication took place between Christine, her mother, and occasionally her grandmother, who formed a formidable trio in support of the lecturing Irishman.

Wilfred was a deputy headmaster at a school in Sheffield and had been a physical training instructor in the Royal Air Force throughout the 1939–1945 war. I used to play tennis with Wilfred regularly on my visits to Yorkshire. I was never quite sure if it was better for me to win such contests or lose them bearing in mind my developing plans for the future of his daughter. Christine's mother had a great voice and loved to sing to herself while preparing food, doing chores around the house, or even sitting, which she rarely did, in a lawn chair in summer sunshine. Christine played the piano and I liked to sing so we would often participate in an impromptu concert around the piano.

As time progressed and we entered the summer of 1960, notions of marrying each other grew rapidly and plans were laid to ensure that Wilfred would give his blessing to the nuptial event. And so it transpired that on a hot summer's afternoon without a breath of wind and with the birds singing in the treetops, Wilfred and Jasper were reclining in adjacent lawn chairs in the back yard of the Savage home with no other member of the family within sight or, presumably, earshot. Soon having exhausted a discussion of tennis, cricket and even summer vacation, I managed to wax poetic in relation to Mr Savage's only daughter and to express, in no uncertain terms, my undying love for her. I think, at this stage, I was prepared to do anything to ensure that his approval was granted and even grovelling might not have been out of the question. However, the response was favourable and sympathetic and indeed I was led to believe that I might be quite a suitable son-in-law if everything unfolded as it should. And so it was that after this prolonged tête-à-tête, it was left to the women in the family to complete the mopping-up operations and some months later, to lay down the detailed plans for the big day.

It transpired that during the war Mr Savage's friends had known him as Pop, and that was the name by which they still would address him. Once I started calling him Pop, life seemed to become very much easier than it had been before and, indeed, Pop and the physicist have been on the best of terms ever since.

Christine's brother, Robert, who was around the age of twelve when we first started courting, was somewhat of an embarrassment whenever I would visit overnight or for a weekend as he insisted upon a share of whatever action there was at such times. As a result, I used to bring with me gifts of a highly educational nature, usually a construction kit that would take several days to complete and which would be all-consuming to a bright lad with creative instincts. This bribery without corruption worked well and by the time the wedding day was approaching everyone in the family was very much on the same team.

When it was determined that formal wear and top hats would be the order of the day at the wedding, I was not at all put out. Indeed the rental of a wedding suit was preferable to the ordeal of buying any other suit that might be in tune with or appropriate for a nuptial occasion of this magnitude. So when I visited a rental company in Birmingham to obtain the requisite article, it was a delight to find that there were many formal suits that would fit me, and a revelation to find out just how large my head, at that particular time, seemed to be in relation to most hats. Having agreed to rent a suit and having determined exactly what size was appropriate, I then thought no more about it until the day before I was due to leave for Sheffield and the grand occasion. En route to the railway station, I called at the rental company and picked up an elegantly sealed box which contained my wedding garments. It was only on the day of the wedding that I discovered that the articles contained in the box were a far cry from those that I had so diligently tried on and approved as appropriate two weeks before. The shock on the morning of the wedding when I put on the rented attire was something for which I had not bargained. The pants were too short and the jacket too large. The hat, fortunately, was up to standard, but overall I felt like a freak on the most important day of my life, and after looking up and down in the mirror for about ten minutes in the morning, decided the only thing to do was to try and carry off the event as best I could in the strange garments that this Birmingham firm had afforded me.

Prior to the wedding, I had stayed overnight in the Rutland Hotel, a delightful if unassuming hostelry, convenient both to Christine's parents' house and the location of the wedding ceremony. My brother, Ian, was the best man, and made sure that I was in good order, fit and well, if not elegantly dressed by the time we went to the church. The Anglican church at Gleadless was situated on the same Ridgeway Road on which Christine's parents lived. The vicar, who rejoiced in the name of Sharpe, was rather high church and I was afraid that some of my Presbyterian relatives (from the North of Ireland) might take exception to the generous dispensing of incense during the ceremony. No such difficulty occurred, and the bridal party dispersed to regroup for the wedding reception in Whirlow Park in glorious sunshine.

Now, if it seems that the wedding ceremony itself has been dismissed rather lightly and briefly in this narrative, it is because the ceremony was and is a blur in my memory, obscured by my acute nervousness on nuptial day. Not that I was unfamiliar with weddings of many kinds and of many faiths. I had, in fact, participated as best man on no less than eight occasions, so there was, in principle, very little that could come as a surprise to me or be unexpected. But, of course, I had never participated in an event that was so totally out of my control or in which I had become so emotionally involved. For whatever reason, the fact of the matter is that I was essentially a gibbering idiot by the time the wedding processional swelled from the organ and my lovely Christine stood beside me before the altar.

I should say, at this stage, in my defence that previously my bride had not been known for her extreme punctuality. I had been known to wait for upwards of an hour for my beloved to arrive at a less demanding location and it may well be that memories of standing in pouring rain for extended periods by the fountains in Birmingham city centre were flashing through my brain as I waited apprehensively at my appointed spot in Gleadless Church.

One interesting feature of the wedding service was that the responses included as an option the traditional phrase 'love, honour, and obey'. Christine opted for the traditional words knowing perhaps that I would never be very good at giving orders nor she particularly keen on implementing them.

Eventually, when all was said and done and confetti had been thrown with abandon at the happy couple, copious photographs were taken by both official and unofficial photographers whose skills did not always match their intentions. The only photograph of the bridegroom and best man taken as a solitary duo was generated against the background of a huge boarding saying 'Polio cripples even the fittest'. And so, on that happy note, the bridal party and guests left for the wedding reception.

The house and gardens at Whirlow looked their best on that fine June afternoon. The lake glistened blue against the background of rhododendrons of many colours and summer was in the air. It was in this romantic environment that I performed my first, in fact only, heroic act as a married man. A vicious wasp, presumably the first of the season, managed to insert itself under Christine's veil and no one seemed to have the faintest idea as to how this problem should be addressed. The physicist, however, in an unaccustomed moment of bravery, squashed the insect between his finger and thumb through the shimmering veil and managed to remove the *corpus delicti* without damage to either bride or veil or, incidentally, injury to the bridegroom. No photographs, however, exist of this heroic incident which may have been more dramatic than artistic.

There was, however, one picture of which I approved and this was of the bride and groom cutting the cake. Being clad as I was in an ill-fitting suit and perfect top hat, there were not too many opportunities for memorable photography. Christine, in her long narrow-waisted flowing white dress with or without her veil, was a picture of beauty and elegance and deserved to have a less Richard III-like bridegroom at her side. The cake-cutting ceremony, however, saved the day and both of us agreed that that picture alone did justice to both of us as we thought we actually were. And so, on to the honeymoon.

It was difficult at the time, and is no less difficult now, to determine how everything went so terribly wrong. I, and I alone, was responsible for the arrangements. Indeed, the whole holiday was kept a secret from the bride until the moment we left Sheffield Midland Station by train for parts unknown. The history of the planning for this event is simply told but difficult to believe.

Some six months prior to the wedding, the mother of the physicist supplied a substantial sum of money to cover the honeymoon. I do not now recall precisely the amount of money involved but as things transpired it was hopelessly inadequate for the overall purpose to which it was put. I had decided, after a visit to Thomas Cook's travel agency in Belfast, that it would be delightful to go by sea on a Union Castle liner from Southampton to the Canary Islands and spend a week or two in Las Palmas before returning in a sister ship to Southampton and the end of the holiday. I booked and paid for the sea trip and an accommodation package and told Christine that the honeymoon was arranged, that it would be a secret, that I would tell her all she needed to know before the day of our wedding actually arrived.

The arrangement sounds absolutely crazy when I think of it now but for some reason or other Christine thought it was quite exciting and went along with the idea. She did not know whether we were going to Skegness or Grimsby or even for a trip on the Grand Union Canal. I did eventually, one week before the wedding, suggest to Christine that she might bring some really summery stuff along with her on her honeymoon and that a little sun lotion might not come amiss if all my plans worked out as anticipated. Now, it should be noted that the dates of the honeymoon were fixed prior to the date of the wedding being finally determined. When I had booked and paid for the honeymoon, I had it fairly clearly in my mind that the dates of the honeymoon would directly follow the wedding, which is the normal procedure. However, the availability of the church and of Whirlow Park finally determined the date of the wedding, and having booked the honeymoon, I failed to concern myself greatly with the final arrangements for the wedding ceremony itself. It therefore came as somewhat of a shock when I discovered in early May that the date of the wedding and the date of the honeymoon were separated in time by ten fine June days. It was too late to change the dates of either wedding or honeymoon and so the immediate task before the physicist was to fill in the intervening period as creatively as possible and without bankrupting the newly founded partnership of man and wife.

The task proved virtually impossible, but at least I can say that twenty years later I had finally paid off the accumulated debt from the honeymoon extravaganza. The only relaxing feature of the overall situation was that I alone knew of the honeymoon arrangements and therefore I was in a splendid position to correct them in a creative and romantic way. So, in the early evening of 16th June, 1960, the physicist and his bride waved goodbye to the relatives and friends at Sheffield Station where they had been unceremoniously bombarded with dahlia heads purloined from the reception at Whirlow and headed for an unknown destination on a train labelled with Birmingham (New Street) as destination. It was not until the train had pulled out of the station that I finally told Christine of the new and improved plan for our honeymoon. We were to travel on the Birmingham train as far as Tamworth. We would then take a taxi from the station cross country to Lichfield, an old cathedral city known as the Mother of the Midlands and spend several days there at the George, which was the finest hotel in the town. Then, we would depart by train for London and Southampton where again we would spend several days at the Avenue Hotel, renowned both for its food and the expansiveness of its accommodations and then, delight of delights, we would finally embark on the *Pendennis Castle* bound for Capetown and Durban but leave the liner at Grand Canary which was its first stop.

Christine was greatly excited at the imaginativeness and the originality of the plan, as was my bank manager both before, during and after the inspired event. The period spent in England leading up to departure from Southampton cost at least fifty per cent more than the entire honeymoon as originally planned. Nonetheless, at this stage, there was nothing to be done but to enjoy every minute of it, which I believe we did. The acute enjoyment did not start however at Tamworth as, unbeknown to the physicist, this station did not possess a taxi rank and Christine and Jasper in their going-away outfits found themselves standing on a deserted station platform at seven o'clock in the evening without even a public telephone to hand. Leaving Christine on the platform with the luggage, luggage I may say for at least three weeks' vacation, I went around the houses nearby until I succeeded in borrowing a telephone and calling a taxi from the nearest town. The taxi arrived about an hour and a half later.

Arriving in Lichfield and at the George Hotel was a pleasant experience after the rigours of the previous couple of hours. The fact that we had essentially missed dinner was not a good omen and the brass knob on the wall of our room that said distinctly 'Ring for the Ostler' made us wonder whether we had slipped back a century or two in time on our journey from Sheffield. Our room was, however, comfortable and well appointed with many modern conveniences. One feature that was anything but convenient was the proximity of the hotel to the cathedral which had a clock chiming the hour and the half hour and, it seemed to us, occasionally the quarter hour, as an indication of the fact that sleep was neither to be expected nor possible.

During our days in Lichfield, we explored the old town and saw the spot at which the last witch to be burnt in England had her comeuppance. We discovered that the people in the heyday of the town had not stood over five feet in height, evidenced by the lintels on the doorways to the older houses, and discovered that the town of Lichfield was home to Joule's Brewery, a family-owned business that had been there for a century at least. The physicist Joule was in fact a member of this brewing family and presumably quaffed the odd glass when not measuring the mechanical equivalent of heat for which he is remembered. The unit of energy in the metric system is now the joule so it was interesting to taste the result of his family's labours in a delightful beverage room known as The Scales. A set of weigh scales was mounted on the front of this public house adding visual reality to the name. The name Joule in the Midlands is pronounced as though it were spelt jowl and the local population was never slow to correct any mispronunciation.

One Monday evening, near closing time, as Christine and I sat down to have a quiet glass of sustenance, a number of large and athletic looking men came into the pub and began to work most industriously over pieces of paper and pints of beer. It transpired that this was the local rugby club and that Monday night was selection night for teams that were to play on the coming Saturday. Two key members of the committee seemed to be prop forwards, being the members of the rugby scrum who support and, in a sense, protect the hooker, the man in the centre of the front row who is entrusted with extracting the ball from among the feet of the opposition's scrum. Anyway, these two prop forwards were clearly key people in the organisation and when closing time was called those present joined them in a circle, and looking inwards chanted together the incantation 'prop, prop, propinquity, meaning togetherness'. On completion of the word togetherness, these huge farmers, if that's what they were, leapt simultaneously into the air with arms outstretched and touched the ceiling. On completion of this unexpected ritual, they clapped each other on the shoulders and moved off quietly into the night. The episode was so short and yet so dramatic that we often recalled it when in similar environment but without the stimulus of Lichfield rugby club. Propinquity is a nice word and undoubtedly does mean togetherness and it was perhaps because we were on our honeymoon that the incident made such a lasting impact. The following day, however, we were off to Southampton.

The journey to the port city was uneventful and we found our hotel without any great difficulty. We explored the docks and watched the great ships. Time in Southampton went by quickly enough. The hotel was very attractive, the food was good and the entertainment excellent. However, once the delights of sniffing the salt air and inspecting ships both great and small, had been sampled we were undoubtedly ready to take part in the honeymoon part two. The *Pendennis Castle* was a brand new ship and the flagship of the Union Castle Line. As with many great ships of the period, there was plenty of space for entertainment, sports, dining and carousing. Organised jogging around the deck was beginning to come into vogue and Jasper and Christine participated in everything with a high degree of enthusiasm. We particularly enjoyed playing deck tennis with some of our fellow passengers and overdid it to the extent that we were badly burned on the shoulders by the time we finally reached our destination at Generalissimo Franco Quay in Grand Canary. The Bay of Biscay had been as calm as a millpond and all organised events from the captain's cocktail party to final disembarkation were flawlessly administered. On arrival on the island however, we were somewhat discomfited to find that the Spanish authorities would dispossess us of our passports for the duration of our stay. This, of course, happened to everyone disembarking but for some reason made us feel like stateless persons for the first few days of our visit.

The Hotel Monopol in Las Palmas, where we stayed, was pretty, clean, with a lively restaurant and a variety of Mediterranean food available. The main fish entrée on the dinner menu differed each day, not only in the dish itself but in the nature of the fish served. Colour varied from off-white to red to purple, but on each occasion the offering was called halibut fish. We were eventually led to the conclusion that our Spanish waiter thought that the word 'halibut' was, in fact, the English word for fish and once we had determined that what he said bore no resemblance to what was laid before us, life became fairly simple and we just took whatever he brought.

Now, it might be thought that the physicist had already made enough errors of judgement in relation to his nuptial festivities and honeymoon to cast some doubt on his administrative and planning abilities, but worse was yet to come. The choice of the largest town on the island, Las Palmas, as a base for our honeymoon was an unmitigated disaster. The reason for this was quite simple. The island itself has mountains in the centre which rise, if I recall correctly, to some six or seven thousand feet and effectively separate one end of the island from the other. What the guidebooks did not tell you was that whereas the southern end of the island is continuously bathed in cloudless sunshine, the other end, where we were staying, was covered in almost perpetual cloud. It transpired that the clouds caused by moisture rising from the ocean, rising to cross the mountains, were trapped by the mountains themselves, so that one half of the island was a little too much like England on a bad summer day whereas the other side was essentially subtropical, as it should be. There was, however, a solution to this problem. It lay in arising at an unearthly hour of the morning each day, usually about five o'clock, and travelling from Las Palmas by bus to the far end of the island, a trip of just under three hours, ending in arrival at the deserted beach of Maspalomas (now a major holiday resort) and then in the late afternoon reversing the process and returning in time for dinner to the Hotel Monopol. Travelling in the bus was a very hot and rather smelly activity because of the natural odours emitted by our human and animal companions on the bus. It was not uncommon for a local farmer somewhere en route to decide to move all his belongings from one location to another by bus, without warning. So bedsteads, sideboards, tables, livestock and the occasional rusted bicycle would be loaded on the vehicle without concern for either timetable or space availability. Apart from one occasion on which the bus driver threatened to remove the physicist and his bride from the bus for holding hands in the front seat, apparently a hanging offence in Spain, these daily sojourns to Maspalomas became an uneventful but integral part of life.

The latter part of the journey to the beach was always more welcome than the initial portion. Once beyond the mountains, the colour and variety of countryside changed dramatically becoming more desert-like with palm trees and continuously brilliant sunshine. The beach itself, on arrival, had nothing to offer but perfect sand for miles, palm trees and a little shack that sold snacks and drinks, and rented deck chairs, of all things. These deck chairs turned out to be traps for the unwary because the hinged canopies, which were supposedly fixed above the head, would suddenly drop of their own accord and could inflict a severe blow to the face or the head. Despite the good offices of several supposedly technical wizards associated with the snack shack, this problem was never overcome and the honeymooners were able to boast several minor head injuries in addition to marvellous suntans on their return.

Las Palmas was not a very attractive place to stay in or visit. The harbour was very much a fishing port but the water was contaminated significantly by oil from cargo ships, tankers and ocean liners on their way to South Africa or from far across the Indian Ocean. There were a number of tired little cafés and open-air places of entertainment where flamenco dancing was a feature in the evenings. But, by and large, Las Palmas was a good place to avoid on a honeymoon trip.

When the time came to leave our honeymoon island, the Island of Dogs (the name Canary comes from the Latin word *canis* meaning dog rather than little bird), it was necessary to first recover our passports from the Spanish customs authorities prior to boarding the vessel which was tied up a mile or so along Generalissimo Franco Quay. When we arrived, a little later than we had intended, the office was open but no one was present, although we could hear someone speaking on the telephone in argumentative Spanish in a back room away from the reception area. After waiting patiently for twenty-five minutes or so in which no one else arrived and no one came to see us, the final hour for boarding the vessel was rapidly approaching and the physicist was for once in a state of panic. Not only were we now late, but we were essentially without any means of financial support. I therefore took it upon myself to leap over the reception desk and rummage through the drawer that I seemed to recall held our passports. The box was certainly full to the brim with passports but, after a few minutes of searching, I finally found the particular McKee articles which were then effortlessly removed. After vaulting back over the desk, Christine and I ran like bats out of hell to the gangplank, eventually to arrive back home in England. Fears that the Spanish authorities might discover the loss of our passports and apprehend us prior to cast-off from the jetty were unfounded and a short time later we were at sea en route for Southampton.

That evening, a special cocktail party was held by the captain to which we were invited, and some of the most delicious hors d'oeuvres that I have ever tasted were consumed. Floods of champagne appeared and we commented to the captain on the excellence and generosity of the shipping line in arranging this coming home party for us. His response was that we should make the most of it while it lasted because the shipping line would certainly recover all its costs in the next couple of days as they were expecting 'a hell of a blow in the Bay', as he put it. Our ship for the return leg of our journey was the *Stirling Castle*, one of the older ships in the line, and considerably smaller and less well appointed than the *Pendennis Castle*.

It was fairly early the next morning when the wind first started to blow and it was somewhere in the middle of the Bay of Biscay where the ship suddenly popped out of the water like a cork and fell back down on its side, breaking most of the portholes above the water line on the port side. The Bay of Biscay, as it is explained to me, is almost semicircular in its geography, as seen from a westerly direction. Therefore, the prevailing westerly wind, particularly when it is blowing at storm force twelve or higher, forces water into this semicircular reflector which then rebounds to the focus in the centre of the bay at which all waves converge. The argument was, and as far as I know still is that when our ship was virtually at the focal point of this concave mirror, the combination of the ship's forward motion, the fierce winds, and the reflected waves was such as to lift the vessel entirely clear of the water after which she dropped inelegantly on her side. The storm lasted virtually until our arrival in Southampton. During this time only five passengers on the ship turned up for every meal, I was one of these. But to say that I enjoyed anything that I ate would be totally incorrect. Plates would only remain on the table if the tablecloths on which they sat were continually swilled with water to give them some traction. The menu on each occasion was limited, to say the least, and the appetites of those few hardy souls who made it to breakfast, lunch, or dinner were scarcely of the ravenous variety that they had been on the outward journey.

Christine, with the best will in the world, was unable to leave her bunk, and whereas the physicist was able to return with a few crackers or a piece of fruit from time to time, these stayed largely uneaten. Final arrival in England was not only a triumph of seamanship for the crew but a tremendous relief to the honeymooning McKees. It is perhaps as well, on reflection, that a honeymoon usually occurs only once in a lifetime. Too much excitement cannot be good for anybody.

The author at a tender age.

Graduating Honours Class Physics, 1952, Queen's University, Belfast.

The author as President of the Students Representative Council, Queen's University, Belfast, annual dinner, 1953.

Delegates to the annual Canadian accelerator conference, Saskatoon, 1983. Author: centre, front row.

The author lecturing at an international conference in Vienna, 1984.

The author (director) and staff of the cyclotron laboratory, 1985.
Author, front row, fifth from left.

The author and his wife Christine in Barbados, 1989.

Meeting to mark the retirement of Prof. B. H. Brandsen, University of Durham, September 1991. Prof. Brandsen, the author's PhD supervisor: front row, centre. The author: back row, third from left.

Chapter Eleven

The Physicist Visits Oxford in Winter

There is no descriptive word in the English language that conveys less useful information than the word 'new'. It imparts no historical fact and is of transitory significance. If a town is named Newcastle, and such towns exist in several countries, this could indicate that at one time a castle was built where the town now stands, or, alternatively the name might have been adopted for obscure connotations with another town at another time, perhaps even in another country.

A well-known hostelry in central London, by the Haymarket, is called The Captain's Cabin. Its walls are wildly festooned with prints depicting the new frigates, wonderful ships from the end of the age of sail and at the dawning of the era of steam. It is difficult to attribute a year to such ships and the word 'new' does little to help.

New College Oxford is an academic institution in much the same boat. Centuries ago it was new (in 1379, to be specific), but the description scarcely seems appropriate today.

While attending a nuclear physics conference in Oxford one January in the late 1950s there was something new and welcoming and contemporary afoot at New College. It was the introduction of central heating, a more than welcome addition to the comforts of university life as perceived by several hundred visiting scientists. The system was 'new', efficient and appropriate – a new utility for a far from new institution. New College had finally entered the twentieth century.

All January conferences in Oxford were Spartan to the extreme. On many occasions British physicists had endured, if not enjoyed, the privilege of staying in an Oxford college in winter when the students had gone down for a vacation break. Of those that I have visited, Keble College was undoubtedly the least appealing. On one occasion, in early January I noted on rising in the morning that the water in the glass by my bedside had accumulated several millimetres of ice overnight. Iced water is normally a welcome beverage to visitors from North America, but not, I think, in such an unexpected situation.

Even today, Keble College has few redeeming features, architectural or otherwise. It is physically unattractive and monastically bleak. On one occasion, Sir Denys Wilkinson was opening a national conference at the college at a time when major external refurbishment was taking place. He stood aloft in the minstrels' gallery and welcomed the delegates below in words somewhat like this, 'I hope you enjoy this conference. On departure for home you may wish to take a souvenir with you. May I suggest a brick or two of Keble College? To assist delegates in this task, the University of Oxford has erected scaffolding all around the college as you will have observed. Help to make Oxford more beautiful! Take a brick or two home with you!'

As a red-brick rather than Oxbridge graduate, I had a peculiar sensitivity to the thinly-veiled pomposity of Oxford University life. I recall on one occasion, again at Keble College, dining in hall with fellow delegates and being served watery soup and a bread roll as an 'appetiser' for dinner. The roll was dry, so I beckoned to a college servant (as they are called), and asked for a little butter for my roll. The immediate response was, 'I would remind the visitor [presumably me] that it is not customary for the young gentlemen [not persons but men] to eat butter at this stage of the meal.'

'I am not a young gentleman!' says I under my breath, 'but would still like some butter.'

The long and short of the tale is that the servant, refreshed by his oratory, moved further up the table, and no butter ever appeared. Guests – paying guests under sufferance – seemed to identify our role at the college.

To confirm my long established view that Oxford University was 'in the world but not of it', an incident took place in the late 1950s, now etched in memory. Nuclear physics was a major field of study in Britain, and a national conference was held, again in the winter, at the Atomic Energy Research Establishment (AERE) at Harwell. Accommodation for the conference was available at colleges in Oxford, and many of us were lodged for one reason or another at Balliol. Buses ferried delegates daily to and from Harwell. All went well until the night of the banquet which was held at the research establishment. After the dinner and speeches, buses took the visitors back to Oxford and hopefully to their beds. However, on arrival at Balliol College some minutes after eleven o'clock in the evening, we found the college as securely bolted and barred as the Tower of London. Our party comprised thirty or so persons from all over the United Kingdom, and as it so happened Sir John Cockroft was among the group. Now whether he was staying at the college or merely talking with members of the group is unclear. What did become clear was that he was determined to solve our problem, and to do so he used a public telephone to call the porter's lodge and hopefully gain admission. The preliminary results of this manoeuvre were not encouraging. The porter indicated that his instructions were to lock the college entrance at 11 p.m. each night during vacation. He appreciated the visitors' predicament, but had no authority to depart from his orders as laid down. Sir John then requested that the porter put him through to the Master of the College who was a personal friend. The Master, it then transpired, was highly unavailable, being at an unknown (to the porter at least) address somewhere in the continent of Africa. Sir John became more and more impatient, and the college servant continued to be quite immovable. Eventually, however, another senior luminary at Balliol College was contacted, and was able to negotiate a solution to the problem. At twelve midnight, and for five minutes only, the main door to the college would be opened to allow entrance to the visitors. The fact that twenty-five minutes remained before the hour of twelve seemed unimportant, so the thirty or so guests of the college huddled together outside in frosty temperatures until the porter saw fit to exercise his authority and implement the agreed solution. On the stroke of twelve midnight the door was opened, and five minutes later was firmly shut.

Long-standing memories are made of such bizarre incidents.

Chapter Twelve

The Physicist at the University of California, Berkeley

Nothing would in the end change our lives more fundamentally than the first year's leave spent at Berkeley California in 1966–1967. The Lawrence Radiation Laboratory, as it was then called, acted as host to many international scientists, and in my case augmented my Fulbright scholarship and salary with an allowance of eight dollars per day for my year's work. Christine and I sailed to New York on the SS *America* in the late summer of 1966 and then travelled by Amtrak to Chicago and then Oakland. Our children, Conor and Siobhan, were just reaching the ages of four and one respectively and enjoyed every minute of the fussing and attention they received on the journey. The house which we rented on Oxford Street in Berkeley was delightful, with plenty of space for children and a playpen, and with adjacent parks that were to be part of daily life for the coming year. The smell of eucalyptus, the tree-rich streets, and Tilden Park with its delightful carousel, bathing beach and little train, all played a part in the memories of that time. Flower power of course was rampant and beautiful people were everywhere. Telegraph Avenue played home to the weird and the wonderful and San Francisco watched us from across the bay. Music and perpetual summer were everywhere.

From the research point of view nothing could have been more refreshing or exciting. It seemed that anything and everything was possible. New discoveries of real or pseudo particles and elements seemed daily occurrences and theoretical ideas from quark models to exact three body calculations were there for the investigation.

Most of my work was carried out at the 88" cyclotron laboratory where I first became familiar with polarisation studies. Rolf Slobodrian's group with which I was associated did some pioneering work in studying and understanding the diproton system, and in searching for non-existent states of helium three. Both then and later, on my return in 1972, few body problems were the focus of most research carried out by the group, although Rolf Slobodrian had by then taken up an appointment at l'Université Laval in Quebec City in Canada.

The group's offices, if they can be so called, were to be found in a hut just behind the 88" cyclotron laboratory proper, boasting a metal roof. Air conditioning was supplied by running water from a hose over this roof on hot days, and by keeping all doors and windows open. The laboratory itself was situated about a third of the way up 'the hill' as it was called and presented a fine view of the Berkeley campus of the University of California. Directly below the cyclotron building were two fraternity houses at base level, and just beyond them and to the left, the Greek Theatre and the university stadium.

This fact relates loosely to a memorable day at the laboratory when a new beam stop weighing around a thousand pounds arrived for installation. Bernard Harvey as Director was taking a healthy interest in proceedings as the forklift truck carrying the object made its way slowly around the outside of the building at cliff top towards the back entrance to the cyclotron. Now, whether the driver of the forklift was overacting, or whether he was merely going too fast on the curve, the result was the same, disaster. Slowly but inexorably the truck began to tilt and the cargo to shift. Being cylindrical in shape the beam stop was a natural roller. It leapt the six-inch concrete rail lining the road and disappeared rapidly downhill towards a fraternity house where it finally came to rest. There was a horrified silence from the bystanding group up above. Bernard Harvey, however, showing statesmanlike aplomb turned to George, the unfortunate driver, with the words, 'George, would you mind going down to the frat house and asking for our bomb back?'

Life at the 88" laboratory was always interesting and often entertaining. The technical support was superb, and the scientists working there, great fun to be with. We got to know the Slobodrians, the Cernys and the Hendries best. Joe Cerny was a group leader shortly to become chairman of the chemistry department at U.C. Berkeley while Dave Hendrie would later become director of the Maryland Cyclotron Laboratory. Not only were the visitors from England made welcome but we were to share many memorable moments at their homes and at points around the San Francisco Bay area, from Joe DiMaggio's at Fisherman's Wharf to Tilden Park and San José.

*

The Few Body Group hut, as I described it earlier, was featureless, with only half a dozen desks and several calculators to give it character. Being outside, and to the back of the laboratory proper, it sat on the edge and side of a canyon, Blackberry Canyon, through which a narrow path led to the science library building. It was not uncommon while walking along this path through the eucalyptus trees to meet deer and then decide who should claim right of way. On one occasion a deer actually entered our hut as a voluntary act of sociability, but that was unusual.

At night, when performing experiments in the laboratory, all was comparatively peaceful. If things were running smoothly you could catch up on recent literature while completing your shift. At other times, when there was to be a beam energy change or a temporary shutdown, time might be spent around the control room while the technical staff produced a beam of the specifications required. Aesthetically a remarkable feature of the view from the control room was that lights on control panels blended at night into the view from the hill down University Avenue and across to the Golden Gate Bridge. The control panels ended in a clear glass window and by night the flickering lights of both control room and city blended into one seamless web of colour.

It was after one overnight run, the third such in a row, that I missed my first earthquake. A severe series of tremors on the Hayward fault occurred as I was driving home from the hill for breakfast at around eight thirty in the morning. My wife, Christine, had to experience falling crockery and flying books from shelves in the house, while a combination of drowsiness and my pneumatic tyres kept me oblivious to the seismic activity around and about. The quake was over by the time I reached home, relaxed and hungry.

Holidays from the laboratory were always an opportunity to see new places and visit new scenes. A long weekend in Yosemite Valley and a similar trip up the Napa Valley later in the year broke up the continuous seven-day work schedule that everyone wished to maintain. Research and vacation were always tackled with the same enthusiasm. One day, several months after arrival at Lawrence Berkeley Laboratory, I was leaving the laboratory at the end of the day when one of my colleagues shouted to me, 'See you on

Monday,' and left. Well, it was Thursday evening so I asked Rolf what was meant by that? It transpired that the following day was Lincoln's birthday and a laboratory holiday to boot, but the knowledge came too late for me and my family to take much advantage of three days' vacation. Nonetheless, I learnt to obtain a copy of the laboratory calendar with high days and holidays included. Next holiday date was marked as Washington's birthday, commemorating another famous American, so I made advanced arrangements to visit the spectacular Lassen Park in northern California with its sulphur pots and fumaroles and resort accommodations. When the day previous to this date arrived, I packed up my books and calculations and wished everyone a good weekend. My colleagues looked surprised. 'Will you not be here tomorrow?' they asked.

'No, of course not, it's Washington's birthday,' I said, somewhat unconvincingly in my defence.

'But we had a holiday on Lincoln's birthday this year,' a colleague explained. 'We celebrate Washington's next year. If you look at the end of the calendar you will see that certain holidays occur only on alternate years!' And so it was! As a result, I was absent without leave to enjoy one of the more delightful, hot and colourful weekends of my lifetime, while the rest worked.

Chapter Thirteen

The Physicist as a Babysitter

While in Birmingham I would rarely babysit for other people's children. I had too much fun on occasions looking after my own. A young Irish student, a red-haired woman from one of the halls of residence, would look after our cherubs, Conor and Siobhan, on those occasions on which Christine and I were invited out socially. The children really enjoyed Kate Jackson's visits and could not get their parents out of the house quickly enough when she was due for the evening.

I had, of course, been known to take care of fellow physicists' children from time to time, particularly before ours were born, but it was not an undertaking that I ever sought. On arrival in Berkeley, California, in 1966 the situation was suddenly different. We had no family or close friends around, and it was therefore a delight to discover that visiting scientists had formed a babysitting club, and that anyone on the approved list could be called for action at a moment's notice, if he or she was available. A points table was kept, and each member was expected to repay owed sittings as quickly as possible, in fairness to others. And so it was, in January 1967 that the McKees had a deficit of two sittings, and I volunteered to redress the balance personally while Christine took care of our own little darlings at our house on Oxford Street.

The first experience was simple, if disturbing. A visiting professor and his wife, rejoicing in the unlikely name of Dadd, had a pair of twins who were headbangers. That is to say that these two kids would put themselves to sleep by banging their heads against the bedhead or the wall as the case might be. My instructions were to leave them alone and all would be well, and so it transpired. I am still not able to decide whether the hammer blows dealt by these young heads were more unnerving than the deathly silence that fell one hour later. On the Dadds' return I was both delighted and surprised to discover that my charges were still alive. My decision in future to avoid headbangers was, however, firm.

And so we come to my second sitting, as it were. This time a rather urbane American scientist and his wife were at the door to meet me as I arrived. They had rented a rather elegant property one block off Telegraph Avenue in an area populated by druggies and undesirables after nightfall.

I found the house with little difficulty. The long lounge that ran through the house from front to back had a large floor-to-ceiling picture window facing the road. Flush with the plate glass window, with arms and legs in a diagonal cross shape, was the older 'baby' aged eleven with his mouth open and tongue stuck out as a permanent greeting to the sitter.

My misapprehension at the evening's mission was immediately accentuated by some words of warning from the parents of this delightful child. He was, it appeared, likely to take advantage of a babysitting person, by slipping noxious substances, animals and plants into the refrigerator once their back was turned. He would tell lies about everything, so the best thing to do was ignore him. His sister, on the other hand, aged six, seemed quite angelic as she disassembled what I assume was a toy gun in the corner.

As the parents left the house they told me one more interesting fact. The previous babysitter had apparently visited the downstairs washroom immediately after the parents' departure. Unbeknownst to him, the key had been removed earlier by the eleven year old who instantly locked the door from the outside. The would-be babysitter was still held in solitary confinement when the parents returned at 2 a.m. He was virtually a gibbering idiot when released. I decided that however great the need, for this evening washrooms were out!

One helpful instruction left me was to make sure the kids, already in their pyjamas, went to bed at 8 p.m. If they refused to go I was to stand firmly in front of the television screen blocking their view, and then with one dramatic move, switch the instrument off. Then, they assured me, the little angels would slowly and reluctantly proceed to bed. For some time watching the television set did not seem to have the same attraction as removing the rugs from the polished wooden floor and then sliding on cushions, at great speed, towards the picture window. However, eventually both sat alert and together on a little coffee table, square with four sharp corners, in front of the television set. All seemed well. At eight o'clock, precisely as instructed, I suggested that it was time for good children to go to bed. Nothing happened, so I resorted to emergency plan A. I stood between the set and the viewers, blocking the screen. Then in one flamboyant movement I switched the television set off.

What happened next is not precisely clear. Certainly both children leapt into the air in disgust. I rather think that the boy then sat down heavily and abruptly on his end of the table which then resulted in the other end shooting upwards as the little girl had not resumed her seat. In any case, a sharp corner of the table struck the nape of the girl's neck which began to spout blood as if it would never stop.

Panic stations ensued. Towels soaked in cold water were applied in quantity, some antiseptic lotion was found, the bleeding slowed but did not stop. The babysitter had no idea what to do next. The address book by the telephone did not boast a list of paediatricians, surgeries or hospitals as is normally the case in a private home. Leaving the children in search of help was clearly not the thing to do so I telephoned my wife at home, prefacing my remarks with 'Darling you are not going to believe this.'

Christine, as always, was the tower of strength. She called our newly found personal paediatrician and at 10 p.m. got helpful advice. 'Keep doing what you are doing. Watch her carefully in bed for at least two hours. Call back urgently if she is sleeping too deeply or starts twitching.'

So I spent the two hours until midnight monitoring the child, interrupted frequently by big brother's encouraging sentence, 'I know she is going to die.'

By midnight she was sleeping peacefully and the bleeding seemed to have stopped. A sterile dressing taped in place made the patient look less severely injured, so the physicist/babysitter sat down to await the arrival of the parents. When they floated in at 3 a.m., two hours late, they asked me 'How did it go?'

'Please sit down,' I said, and then told them the whole gruesome story.

When I had finished the father said, 'Well, she is all right now, so that is the main thing. Thanks for babysitting!' When I left, no one had checked the children, and no surprise or concern had been exhibited. I went home to my dear wife and children and went to bed. Later I heard from another visiting professor and his wife that I had been highly recommended as a babysitter by this very pair. No thank you, says I.

Chapter Fourteen

The Physicist Goes to the University of Manitoba

> My girl's from Winnipeg,
> She's got a wooden leg,
> Made from a whiskey keg,
> etc.

These words of timeless poetry from the Ulster Students' Songbook (1954) comprised my entire knowledge of Winnipeg prior to 1967 when I visited Canada for the first time. It is not now clear whether I thought at that time that Winnipeg was a village or a city, or indeed that it was situated in Canada. However, in late 1972 an advertisement in an international scientific journal brought that city front and centre to my attention.

The physics department of the University of Manitoba in Winnipeg was conducting a search for a Senior Professor of Nuclear Physics to be charged with responsibility for the research programme of the 50 MeV Spiral Ridge negative ion cyclotron in that location. It encouraged interested parties to communicate directly with the department chair, Dr A.H. Morrish, and submit a career history to date.

The interesting feature of the announcement was, to me, the potential capability of the Manitoba cyclotron as compared to the Birmingham Radial Ridge machine with which I had struggled for several years following my sabbatical leave at Berkeley. Limited as the Birmingham facility was to single energy operation and deuteron acceleration, it was only the sophistication of the ion sources and the targets used with it that made the Radial Ridge machine in any way competitive. Polarised ion source design and a polarised helium-three target had recently increased the life expectancy of the facility, but it was still frustrating to compete with variable energy machines elsewhere. The Manitoba accelerator on the other hand had obvious advantages. Variable energy was one. Negative ion acceleration enabled extraction energy to be varied merely by altering the position and angle of a stripping foil. Axial injection of beams from an ion source to magnet centre was necessary prior to conducting polarisation studies, but the man capable of initiating such a program was already in Winnipeg, Saewoon Oh, a Korean physicist who had already performed heroically for the cyclotron group at Birmingham. So, whereas polarised beams and a polarised target already existed in Birmingham, the potential for developing a highly competitive laboratory lay in Winnipeg, thanks to the energy range and variability of the local negative ion facility.

Having expressed some interest in the Manitoba appointment and submitted a curriculum vitae in support of my interest, nothing transpired for about a year. However, in late 1973 that situation changed. I was invited out to Winnipeg to meet the staff and graduate students of the physics department and to give a colloquium and a research talk. The trip took place in early February, by air from Heathrow airport direct to Winnipeg. The flight took around eight hours on a stretched DC8, flying the polar route. This fact made Winnipeg seem close to England; much nearer in practical terms than it is in winter today, with most flights funnelled through Toronto.

I was met at the airport by Allan Morrish, the long-time chair of the department. My welcome was warm and Morrish was extremely helpful in relation to all components of my visit. He made it quite clear that should everything turn out well and I agreed to come to Manitoba, I would exceed expectations if the cyclotron laboratory survived as a research unit for three years, the funding agency, then AECB, being about to pull the plug on the facility. It was however necessary, in addition, for me to be interviewed at Atomic Energy of Canada Laboratories at Chalk River, Ontario, by Geoffrey Hanna, Chair of the Funding Committee of AECB, in order to acquire the necessary good housekeeping seal of approval for my appointment and guaranteed funding. Both the visit to the University of Manitoba and that to Chalk River seemed to go as well as might be hoped for, bearing in mind that I had never before met most of the people involved. Also the local staff were not necessarily feeling unthreatened by the advent of a non-Canadian physicist with a totally European background as of that date. The situation in the physics department was an interesting one. It was part of an isolated university but almost independent in its ability to design and fabricate structures essential to the development of the cyclotron facility. There were some good nuclear physicists, but others lacked confidence in their own abilities to design research programmes and work independently. Some faculty members with considerable skills were either uninvolved in accelerator research and development or seen as irrelevant to the future plans for the facility. Frictions within the physics staff at the time were considerable. Morrish was regarded as autocratic, domineering, and, on occasion, quite nasty to colleagues. He was however a good physicist and could certainly speak and act for his department which was helpful to me at this time of transition. Another physicist, Robin Connor (Robert D. Connor), currently Dean of Science, who had visited me in Birmingham when my translation to Winnipeg had been originally mooted, continued to be supportive. I was also familiar with the work of one local physicist, Wim van Oers, and at the time many of my interests were similar to his. We never, however, collaborated closely on any project, and he became increasingly involved in the evolving TRIUMF laboratory in Vancouver.

An immediate concern on visiting Manitoba was that the small number of theoretical physicists in the department seemed individually isolated in their own areas of expertise. This was quite unlike the unity of purpose of all theorists in Birmingham and their close association with experimental research programmes. In the twenty years following my eventual move to Winnipeg, all that has changed. The arrival of new young blood in Osborn and later Southern and the formation of an Institute for Theoretical Physics finally broke down many of the barriers to co-operation, interpretation and understanding, making new ideas and mathematical methods widely available to anyone needing them or open to such changes.

On my return to Birmingham, Christine and the children were anxious to know how everything had turned out. What are the houses like? Is Winnipeg a large city like Birmingham? These turned out to be difficult questions to answer. I don't know that I was inside a house at any time. I had stayed in the Montcalm Gordon Motor Hotel and had been entertained at several delightful restaurants as well as at the university. All I could recall was that everything was white; roads, houses, everything. I rather thought that most people lived in single family dwellings and that few homes were the same as or even similar to each other. I did recall someone telling me that the size of Winnipeg was greater than inner Los Angeles. However, I also knew its population to be around six hundred thousand so there were no simple answers to straightforward questions.

Largely because the time seemed right for a move if one was to be made, neither of the children yet being in English 11-plus education, and with our experiences of Berkeley, California, Heidelberg, Budapest, and several other European laboratories behind us, we decided almost overnight to accept the challenge. While Christine finished up her work at the Centre for Urban and Regional Studies at Birmingham University and began packing, I thought in depth about my initial moves on arrival in Winnipeg.

In this activity I was greatly assisted by insights and pen portraits of personalia at Manitoba from John Nelson, at that time a research associate and now a research professor at the University of Birmingham. He had recently returned from a year spent at Manitoba as a research associate. He was able to describe people in such detail, and their academic and technical strengths with such accuracy that I had a full working team both in my head and in my diary by the time I arrived in Canada. My own knowledge of Saewoon Oh's abilities as an accelerator physicist and of the operating structure required to run a major facility made my initial moves on arrival unusually interesting, both to the personnel involved and to the funding agency. It was most fortunate that there were several recent MSc graduates of unusual technical ability not wishing to proceed further academically, but requiring challenging full-time employment. Irving Gusdal became cyclotron superintendent, assisted by Al McIlwain and later Robert Pogson, Vladimir Derenchuk and Damien Gallop. John Bruckshaw was a methodical and reliable draftsman, Wally Mulholland was the in-house vacuum specialist and stores and equipment manager, and Jim Anderson was a real asset with his computer science background and hardware skills. These skills were complemented by the software abilities of

Tony Smith. Between them, over a period of fifteen years, the non-academic support staff of the cyclotron facility themselves published a significant number of useful papers in refereed scientific journals and made presentations at many international conferences. Some time later my research group was enhanced by the arrival of Jim Birchall whose PhD programme I had supervised in Birmingham, and students Chris Randel and Matthew (M.S.A.L.) Al-Ghazi whom I had taught there as undergraduates.

At this time the mechanical and electrical workshops of the department of physics, with a staff of about a dozen people, could fabricate and repair almost anything. The axial injection system installed in 1975, the new DEE systems for both negative hydrogen and deuterium, a high energy microprobe, and all magnets built after 1978 were completely designed, constructed and commissioned in-house, with little assistance even from local firms. We were in every sense happy to be independent of manufacturers in the larger centres in central Canada and the United States. Harnessing Francis Konopasek, our resident RF expert and Bill Uzat from the electrical workshop as a team with a long range programme, enabled the cyclotron to be converted from push-pull to push-push mode thereby improving both energy variability and beam quality. The hardware for conversion to single turn extraction for deuterons was completed just as the laboratory finally lost infrastructure funding from NSERC (the Natural Sciences and Engineering Research Council) in 1988.

In many ways the idea of having a Machine Development Group working quite independently but in support of the research programme, faculty and students, meant that everyone moved ahead together. The development of a high energy proton induced X-ray emission (PIXE) analysis system at the cyclotron also meant that there was always a short duration experiment of value to slot in when a longer nuclear physics experiment broke down, or a break in operation was requested by a research team. Twenty-four hours per day, seven days a week running was in place from 1976 to 1985. Within that time period, for a three-year spell, the laboratory supplied several radiopharmaceuticals to hospitals across Canada. Every Tuesday morning, for example, radioactive Iodine 123, not otherwise available in Canada, was supplied to patients requiring thyroid scans, as far away as Halifax and Edmonton. For this system to work, the irradiated material from the cyclotron laboratory, after production on Tuesday morning was shipped to the Health Sciences Centre radiochemistry centre for separation, final production and quality control. The final product was then shipped out on regular Air Canada flights to purchasers. In Halifax patients were booked for scans using the material every Wednesday morning.

In retrospect it is interesting to note that private sector and external bodies did not believe that an academic institution could reliably give such a not-for-profit service. This we did however, missing only two deliveries in the first two years. The supply of radiopharmaceuticals to the public ended when AECL Commercial Products entered the same market. We then withdrew our public service, returns from which had in fact barely covered its own direct costs. Dr Ian Sutherland, Head of Radiology at that time, and Dr Mervyn Billinghurst deserve great credit for participating in this outlandish project while it lasted. All who were involved in producing radioactive iodine will recall the excitement of our first production batch which was actually shipped to Vancouver by Air Canada. So far so good! Unfortunately, someone forgot to unload the sample from its storage spot in the wing of the aircraft, with the result that when it was finally tracked down it had been halfway around the world and was to all intents and purposes, dead as the dodo.

The nuclear research programme of the laboratory covering polarisation studies, total reaction cross section measurements, high resolution analysis of scattering experiments, high energy proton PIXE and few body problems is well documented in the Annual Reports of the Cyclotron Laboratory and in the several hundred scientific publications relating to it. The scientific output of the laboratory was excellent to the end. Dr Gary Smith, a particle physicist, and Guy Durocher, a computer scientist made valuable contributions in the latter years.

If asked what was the greatest administrative achievement of my years as director of the cyclotron laboratory it would undoubtedly be my ability to ensure that Jovan Jovanovich, the stormy petrel of the physics department would publish in a highly regarded journal the technique and results of his massive p-p Bramsstrahlung experiment completed several years prior to my arrival. I succeeded, somehow, and Jovanovich has, in one way or another, been publishing continuously since that time.

In retrospect, one of the interesting and socially integrating features of my earlier life in Birmingham had been the Christmas parties held by the late Sir Rudolf and Lady Peierls for faculty, research scientists and graduate students in mathematical physics. This single initiative seemed to unify that department in a way that no other might have succeeded. It was not so much what was done as how it was done!

So, on arrival at Manitoba, my wife Christine and I attempted to follow the same prescription and throughout the life of the cyclotron as an operating facility, the annual party became a tradition. Of course, all personnel in the laboratory knew each other well, being a tightly-knit group of fifty or so. Nonetheless, the presence of wives, and girlfriends, helped to generate a unity of purpose that might otherwise not necessarily have been present in the group. But this was not the only occasion in the year that personnel would meet together on a social basis. Every time a graduate student obtained a PhD, or a member of support staff went on to greater things, a social event was held. The cyclotron group would meet at noon at the Montcalm Gordon Hotel beverage room, partake of their excellent $2.50 roast beef lunch and have a few beers. The director would give a hopefully appropriate but light-hearted eulogy and then present a parting gift donated by the laboratory as a whole. It was always a well-attended affair. The gifts were always tastefully packaged and adorned by the secretarial staff as a voluntary chore.

Around 1986, someone, I forget who, was leaving, and it was two years or so since the previous lunch of this kind. I suggested that we resume the tradition and have our little lunch. One or two staff wondered where we should hold it? I insisted that we follow the well-established mechanism for such events. This was that precisely at 11.30 a.m. two worthy graduate students would go to the hotel, and take over two tables – always the same ones – in the beverage room. Then around the noon hour the rest of us would arrive and have lunch. The rest of the programme would then proceed as usual. 'If you say so!' said my eager helpers. Now it so happened that on this particular day my eleven o'clock class overran somewhat and I arrived late at around 12.20. Then the enormity of what I had arranged became clear. As an extra feature at lunchtime there was now a stripper! The two tables we always used were next to the dance floor and almost part of the show itself. Well, I tried to proceed as if nothing had happened which was virtually the case until I collected my lunch. Then, as the appropriate stripping music began, I decided to grab a window of opportunity, stand up with my back to the action and deliver a few humorous asides in relation to our departing colleague. I remember nothing of what I said! I was aware only that all eyes were not always upon me, and that the environment was not really conducive to Mark Anthony-like oratory. Nonetheless, apart from one customer, not of our party, who kept shouting 'sit down' all went as well as could reasonably be expected. As I sat down finally, I believe that the official act still had a bra and G-string to remove. This was the last of these highly-charged emotional farewells ever to be held in the beverage room of the Montcalm Gordon Motor Hotel.

Throughout my time as director of the Cyclotron Laboratory, I was fortunate to have the support of several wonderful executive assistant/secretary persons. Pat Rye, who had previously worked for a Lieutenant Governor as personal secretary, looked after everything from paper typing through bookkeeping to acting as receptionist. At the height of our activities in the late seventies the laboratory acquired a full-time secretary in addition, Cindy Roy, who also acted as a rather lovely Easter bunny at the appropriate time of the year. This function was not, however, part of her job description. Later on, after the retirement of Pat, and an appropriate send-off, Jennie Koersvelt gained the hot seat, and kept an efficient eye on grants, bookkeeping and communications until the termination of funding for the accelerator laboratory was in sight.

In retrospect, and despite the rapid dissolution of a highly skilled technical staff, it is clear that everyone in the support staff progressed onward to a successful career in management or technology and took their skills with them.

The cyclotron is now officially mothballed. The equipment is being protected for future activity, but such an event must be unlikely. The cost to reactivate even if the physics warranted it would be prohibitive. The lifelong licence it holds from AECB is however being maintained and protected. Perhaps one day a different phoenix will arise from the ashes. Just prior to the cessation of operations at the University of Manitoba 50 MeV cyclotron, the University of Manitoba purchased from Leo Narodny of the Barbados Optics Company, a 120 keV ion implanter capable of producing a 5 µA beam of argon ions within a 1 mm diameter spot, and of accelerating most light gaseous ions.

This little facility has been extensively used in materials studies since the demise of the big machine, but not only is the physics involved quite different, but the technical support necessary to take advantage of any sophisticated instrument is no longer to be found in the Accelerator Centre (the name adopted ten years ago when the Narodny accelerator was added to the cyclotron as a facility). Nonetheless, Maya Mathur, a sound physicist and expert in Raman light scattering, continues the fight for upgrading and maintenance of the ion implanter and excels in the training of students.

Chapter Fifteen

The Physicist Recalls Anecdotal Tales of the Cavendish Laboratory as Told in Cambridge in 1982

In September of 1982 a conference was held in Cambridge to celebrate the fiftieth anniversary of the discovery of the neutron by Sir James Chadwick. Now, whereas the summary and visionary papers presented were of high quality and stimulating to members of the neutron physics community, the commemorative session held in the Guildhall on Sunday afternoon was in many ways the most memorable part of the entire event.

Bill (W.E.) Burcham FRS, a former student of Chadwick's at Cambridge, and Oliver Lodge, Professor of Physics at the University of Birmingham, and for many years a guide and mentor to the physicist, introduced and integrated a lively series of vignettes presented by those who had either worked with or known James Chadwick well.

John Radcliffe, an eminent medical scientist, recalled the dingy and dirty, if not dismal, building in Free School Lane that was the Cavendish Laboratory of the Thirties. It was built originally in 1874 as a gift from Chancellor Spencer

Compton Cavendish of the University of Cambridge. Cavendish was a direct descendant of Henry Cavendish, a physicist best known for discovering that water is not an atom but a molecule, and for weighing the earth in the privacy of his own laboratory. Henry Cavendish, who died in 1811, had published little of his extraordinary work in a variety of fields of physics including electricity, He had attended Cambridge University but never taken a degree and had become a Fellow of the Royal Society in 1760 despite the apparent drawback of not having any academic qualification to his name.

Experimental physics laboratories at universities worldwide were virtually non-existent when the Cavendish was established and when Clark Maxwell, as Professor of Physics, had the opportunity to name the new laboratory in Free School Lane, he insisted that it take the name of Cavendish and that the collected works of Henry Cavendish be at long last published and made available to the scientific community.

The achievements of the Cavendish Laboratory in various branches of physical science are notable and memorable. Many of them relate directly or indirectly to the discovery of the neutron in 1932. For example, the availability of and understanding of the properties of zinc sulphide impregnated with 1:10,000 of copper ensured that Sir Ernest Rutherford could carry out his memorable experiments on splitting the atom.

Another eminent physicist, C.T.R. Wilson of the Cavendish Laboratory, was a known mountain climber and observed, on climbing to abnormal heights, that droplets of water formed in a way that they did not at lower levels and found that there was a compression ratio in the atmosphere between 1.3 and 1.4 at which water first formed on positive hydrogen ions and then at higher pressure on negative ions. Indeed, at a compression ratio of 1.5:1 both of these ions effectively formed nuclei on which water would condense, and this fact was invaluable in generating the cloud chambers of which the Cavendish made so much use in later years.

In the early Thirties, electronic components available for scientific research basically involved thermionic valves, and it was the discovery by Marconi Pye of a new valve in which the anode and the grid could be brought out at different sides of the device that made possible the amplification of weak electronic signals that could not have been observed before. It was Rutherford's people who decided to underrun the filament of such a valve and discovered that they could remove all inherent noise, effectively detecting signals from real processes that previously would have been unobservable.

Rutherford, being a naturally impatient man, would proceed with whatever tools were at his disposal and came to hand. His work on alpha particles and the disintegration of the nucleus depended entirely on the three unlikely pieces of information just outlined. For this reason, the improbability of the development of nuclear physics was the topic of discussion for Vivian Bowen, who not only had been a student of Chadwick's but more recently had become a peer of the realm.

The difficulty encountered in minimising electronic noise from a single element was enhanced when electronic circuits became available and operational. Small vibrations or disturbances could inhibit completely the operation of such equipment. In the early Thirties, with Rutherford as Director of Research at the Cavendish, it became normal to keep a close lookout for the arrival of the great man in the laboratory. Vivian Bowen had taken it upon himself to erect a substantial and highly visible notice saying, 'Speak softly, please'. This was erected at the entrance to the nuclear physics laboratory when it was believed Rutherford was about to visit. Rutherford was not only a big man but had a very big voice, and all he had to do was say 'Good morning!' for electronic apparatus, that had worked effectively for several weeks, to cease operations altogether. So Bowen and his sign team were essential to the progress of nuclear physics at the Cavendish Laboratory.

Ernest Walton, one of the celebrated team of researchers, Cockroft and Walton, who designed the high voltage linear accelerator necessary for the acceleration of protons to energies required in the artificial disintegration of lithium into alpha particles, recalled how Ernest Rutherford responded to the first fundamental experiment carried out using the accelerator. In order to observe flashes of light from a zinc sulphide screen bombarded by alpha particles, one had to squat in a small dog-kennel-like Faraday Cage protected from the strong electric fields of the accelerator and containing the equipment and microscope necessary for observation of the emitted light. This little kennel was barely adequate for Walton and another student to enter, but for Ernest Rutherford it was a challenge of the greatest proportions. He almost completely filled the available volume. Nonetheless, after a series of precise instructions such as 'lower the voltage', 'increase the current', 'turn off the beam' and 'change the target', Rutherford became convinced that the results were not only observable but repeatable. 'I can recognise an alpha particle when I see one,' he is reported to have said.

The discovery of the neutron was due entirely to the energy and insistence of James Chadwick, who got little personal coverage in the commemorative session. The reason for this seemed to be fairly clear. He was an aloof man, often abrupt or even rude, to whom few people took readily and a man who took less kindly than most to advice of any kind. The only speaker of the afternoon session who could relate with any warmth to James Chadwick the man, was Maurice Goldhaber, then Director of Brookhaven National Laboratory in the United States. Goldhaber recalled that on his arrival at Cambridge as a research associate from Berlin, Chadwick had from the outset been extremely helpful to him. Goldhaber had expected to be a resident of Faversham House, the hostel for graduate students. However, Chadwick suggested that he would be better off in a college where, in Chadwick's words, 'They do things for you.'

And so, on the advice of his guide and inspiration, Maurice went wandering down a street towards first Trinity College, then St John's and finally, Magdalene in search of accommodation. At Trinity they were apologetic but said that all vacancies had been filled many months previously. At. St John's they gave him a form to be completed and undertook to respond within six weeks. On arrival at Magdalene College he filled in a form and, on inspection, the director of accommodation said, 'Ah, you are a refugee. We really should have one of those.' And so Maurice Goldhaber became a resident of Magdalene College. He also received a gift of one hundred pounds from the college towards his annual expenditures. Those were less bureaucratic days!

Graduate students, it seems, had an exciting and invigorating time at the Cavendish Laboratory in the early 1930s. Not that it was easy to become a graduate student. Indeed, to become an experimentalist, it had been necessary for many years to pass a practical techniques test in glassblowing, there being only one qualified glassblower in the laboratory. Soda glass was the medium of most work prior to the Thirties and only then did working with Pyrex become possible and preferable. So in the 1920s all students were required to successfully manufacture a 'cold trap' which required bending and connecting molten glass to other components. I recall that in Queen's Belfast, when I was a graduate student, it was also necessary to show some expertise in making a butt joint in glass in order to proceed with other studies. Most students at Cambridge in the end succeeded in satisfying the instructors and could indeed make a cold trap. There was however one exception. Hartree, of the mean field approximation and other theoretical wonders, never succeeded in becoming an experimental physicist because of his inability to perform this one technical task. Indeed, it was suggested at the commemorative session that graduate students initially or finally failing to make devices with soda glass consumed up to half of the annual budget for the Cavendish Laboratory, a sum that ran to £2,500 in a particular year of that vintage.

As mentioned earlier, during my graduate student life at Queen's University Belfast, the department was festooned with signs saying simply, 'Faraday did it on less'. During Rutherford's reign at the Cavendish Laboratory, an annual budget of £2,500 was sufficient to carry out the work of which we now know so much. On the suggestion that Rutherford should apply for a larger grant for a radioactive source in order to get better statistics and to shorten the time of some of his experiments, he responded that, 'If we do this once, then we will have to account each year for all the work that we do in quite a different way.' And so he never asked for the money for the larger source. 'We don't have the money, so we will have to think,' was Rutherford's motto and it was an ideal to which modern governments in many countries now ascribe and aspire.

Sir Rudolf Peierls, one of the key figures in the Manhattan Project and an active figure at many Pugwash conferences (Pugwash, Nova Scotia), summarised in a qualitative way the theoretical dilemmas that faced physicists in the early Thirties. The year 1932 was some six years after Schrödinger's great contributions to quantum mechanics but prior to the invention of either the nuclear reactor or the atomic bomb. It is hard to imagine, as we approach the year 2000, that there were only two elementary particles known to man at this time, one being the electron discovered by J. J. Thompson of the Cavendish Laboratory just prior to the year 1900, and the proton which was widely recognised as being fundamental to all life as we know it. The idea that the neutron was therefore composed of a positively charged proton and a negatively charged electron was attractive to many people. In an address in response to the presentation of the Göttingen medal, Rutherford once stated that, 'I will believe that there are no electrons in the nucleus when I don't find any', or words to that effect. The discovery of positive electron emission from nuclei in addition to the existence of electrons was a further indication to many people that electrons might possibly exist in the nucleus of the atom. The world of quarks and gluons was a faraway one at that time but neutrons as particles and probes entered centre stage in the decade following the discovery of the neutron.

Sometimes discoveries and ideas develop so quickly in areas of science that it is hard to reconstruct either their development or the interpersonal conflicts that in the end lead to the advancement of knowledge. Sadly, many, if not most of the interpreters of the events of 1932 when the neutron was born have now gone to their reward, and only their scientific papers and anecdotes remain to encourage and inspire the physicists who follow them.

Finally, perhaps the most amusing and respectful reminiscence came from the late Sir Harrie Massey. He recalled that a Mr Lincoln was the marvellously 'conservative' custodian of all equipment in the Cavendish Laboratory. His waxed moustache and cloth cap made him instantly recognisable to all. Cap and man were never apart, except, we are told, when the director, Rutherford, would call on the telephone. Throughout such conversations, Mr Lincoln would stand respectfully, cap in hand, listening to the requests from the great man.

The Cavendish was clearly a fascinating place in the early part of the twentieth century, and memories of the old laboratory in Free School Lane are well worth preserving, particularly now as its destruction seems imminent.

Chapter Sixteen

The Physicist as a Musician

Musical performance is perhaps the arena in which theory and experiment in physics come most synergistically together. Wave length, oscillation, and frequency are all essential to our understanding of melodic form or syncopated rhythm. Physics is the underlying science behind the creative genius of both Mozart and Brubeck. It is almost definitely for this reason that so many physicists are naturally either devoted to music or active participants in the art. Science and Art find their interface in music.

I first discovered music at the age of six when I was sent to classes and almost driven to madness by piano forte instruction that was supposed to make a complete person out of me. My talent for solo instrumental performance was quickly shown to be limited and after determined efforts to play such instruments as the clarinet, drums, classical guitar, electric guitar and the bagpipes, my reputation as a performer was somewhat less than most other artists trying to find a niche for their creative ambitions.

At one stage, however, at the age of seven, my mother determined that I was a natural treble singer and should be encouraged to take part in the Belfast musical festival. To that end I obtained instruction from a far out relative in the art of projecting one's voice, sustaining a note, and basically learning how to sing. I believe that I hated every moment of this exercise. When the great day came and McKee,

Competitor No. 27, had to sing the same piece as everyone before him and everyone behind him at the festival, I stood in the Ulster Hall, in the middle of an empty stage, only to find that my voice had disappeared and that only the merest squeak could be heard by the audience. In addition, the chandeliers in the hall, on which I was fixing riveted attention, seemed to sway and to rotate so that, having completed almost half of my performance, I was saved from further punishment by the thanks of the examiners and an instruction to leave the stage.

Later, however, as a teenager, I became more interested in singing as a voluntary activity. Indeed, Billy McKnight, the organist and choirmaster of Stormont Presbyterian Church, Belfast, took me under his wing and on a weekly basis I would learn and practise songs as varied as those of Warlock, Fauré and Percy French. Nevertheless, as I improved and became earmarked for tenor leads in cantatas and oratorios, my recollection of the Ulster Hall fiasco came more frequently to my mind and I never gave a more than adequate performance of any item in my fairly extensive vocal repertoire.

The same was not necessarily true of my renditions at Saturday night parties or beverage room outings after exhaustive athletic events. Indeed, I rather enjoyed the 'one singer, one song' role that the average Irishman would play in such events.

In addition, my second year at university brought me into contact with a friend, Wolfgang Kiernan, whose mother was German and whose father was Irish. He had considerable fluency as an accompanist and he and I somehow got together to play and sing lieder; in particular, songs by Hugo Wolf and Franz Schubert. Eventually we competed in lieder classes at various festivals around the North of Ireland and, on one occasion, took a busload of supporters to the Ballymena Musical Festival. Knowing no

German myself, I was very much in the hands of his mother, who taught me to sing fluently in Rhenish German. Together Wolfgang and I collected several medals and some notoriety in the two years we were together.

However, to return to the main thrust of this account, I loved music, had no instrumental talent, but was capable, on occasions, when the correct number of pints of bitter had been consumed, to exhibit great feats of memory and of sustained vocal performance. This fact stood me and some of my friends in good stead in late August of 1956, just prior to my departure to the University of Birmingham.

A gorgeous couple of summer weeks in the North of Ireland found a group of friends and I holidaying enthusiastically at Portrush on the North Antrim Coast. Days full of sunshine, swimming, cavorting and occasionally singing had come to an end. The final Friday of August and vacation was upon us. All were due to depart for our homes in Belfast on the Saturday morning, due particularly to the lack of financial wherewithal to continue our stay over the weekend.

'It is a pity,' said Norman Henry, a prominent rugby player in Northern Ireland at the time, 'that we can't stay until Monday as we have nothing in particular to do in Belfast over the weekend.' We all agreed.

'It is a pity we can't acquire a sum of money in the vicinity, of say twenty pounds, to tide at least a few of us over until that time.' We all agreed.

'There is just one chance that we might do so,' said a third member of the group. 'If we were to win the amateur talent contest tonight at the Arcadia Ballroom then two or three of us could afford the hotel bill for the weekend and the problem would be solved.'

'Perhaps we could win the contest,' said another.

'And how do you think we could arrange that?' said a realist among us.

'Well,' said Norman, as I recall the discussion, 'Jasper can sing a mean song whenever he's had a few pints in him. So, perhaps if he concentrates on what he might sing, the rest of us might try to organise a victory.'

Now, crazy as this idea may sound, it seemed much more reasonable within the confines of Gilbey's Snug on Main Street in Portrush prior to venturing forth to the Arcadia Ballroom. Indeed, so eager were my colleagues that I should be mentally undisturbed, that I was left to plan the details of my performance while they arranged to ensure that I was properly received and adequately applauded when the great moment came.

While it is not clear in retrospect at what hour we finally arrived at the ballroom, admission was still allowed and I was ushered on stage by my colleagues to enter for the amateur talent contest. It was somewhat alarming however to find myself seventeenth competitor in the solo performance category, a list to which three additional optimists were added as the night progressed.

Norman, Don, Desmond, Sam and others who may even now recognise themselves, wandered freely around the dance hall expressing general excitement at the anticipated performance of No. 17 in the amateur talent contest. They also distributed themselves, in the manner of a Communist meeting, throughout the hall so that no one was without advance knowledge of Jasper McKee by the time he went on stage, despite the fact that few would ever have heard of him prior to that evening.

Norman, I think it was, gave a final instruction to the performer which involved the scale and nature of the operation. The supporting orchestra was called Dave Glover and His Showband. They had a big band sound and it was anticipated that most of the songs that were delivered would be imitations of those from their own repertoire. Being No. 17 on such a list, this strategy did not seem such a good idea to my friend, Norman.

'You must,' he said, 'I think, do something different.'

And the strategy was then defined. Among my repertoire, if you can call it that, I had several songs that are known in Ireland as come-all-ye's. They are unaccompanied folk songs that have to be delivered with perfect pitch and enunciation and, incidentally, an air of confidence. So it was decided that Jasper McKee, on being called upon as No. 17, would go to the leader of the band and say, 'I would be grateful if you chaps would take a rest. I prefer to sing unaccompanied. The song will be called *A Sailor Courted a Farmer's Daughter.*' The shock, if not arrogance, of this approach to the late stages of competition was intended to concentrate all minds on the singer in hand and as only a couple of late entrants were to follow, all could be won or lost on this decision. As it transpired, it was a long and boring evening for No. 17, seated somewhere by the side of the stage and waiting for his inevitable moment to arrive. By the time No. 16 was in full cry, all effects of alcohol, coercion and friendship seemed to have evaporated.

Nonetheless, on arrival on the stage, I did my part as planned. I thanked the band for their intended efforts but said that I would prefer to sing alone and off I went. I was somewhat surprised, if not delighted, by the response I received on stepping to the microphone. It was as if the many hundred souls present had been my fan club for many years and I got some feeling of what it might be like to be a real celebrity. I sang the song with some confidence and to the delight of my five or six friends. When I had completed my performance, the response was quite unbelievable. People shrieked, clapped, leapt up and down, and even tried to get up on the stage. Order, however, was quickly restored and the final three singers did their pieces.

obviously perturbed by the turn of events, and only the final singing of *The Northern Lights of Old Aberdeen* by a semi-coherent Scot seemed to restore the audience to a sense of normality.

The organisers of the amateur talent contest had determined in advance that the prize money would be awarded on the basis of audience applause. And so they went religiously through all numbers from one to twenty, looking at their applause meter and recording some indecipherable numbers on some unidentifiable pieces of paper. It, of course, transpired that the only number that anyone could remember was No. 17. Whenever No. 17 was mentioned, all hell broke loose and after that it was downhill all the way to the bank, as they say.

I learnt a great deal from this experience, principally that it is not a bad thing to have a little talent but organisation can win the day ninety per cent of the time. I wonder if there is a moral there for physicists and politicians the world over.

In concluding this epic tale, it merely remains to mention the fact that Norman Henry and I managed to stay in our hotel on Mark Street until Monday. It started to rain torrentially on Sunday morning, and by the time we took the train to Belfast on Monday morning, there were virtually no visitors left in the town of Portrush.

The synergy of music and physics in the university environment was first emphasised to me when I arrived in Birmingham some months after my heroic performance at Portrush. The physics department at Birmingham University was supreme in nuclear physics at the time. Scientists from all over the world would make detours to visit the university and I was fortunate to meet some of the leading physicists of the time in the very early days of my new appointment.

Of particular significance to the theme of this chapter was the fact that an inordinate number of members of staff were not only interested in music but instrumental in promoting it. Norman Dyson was a skilled organist who played with the City of Birmingham Symphony Orchestra on more than one occasion. His performances at the organ in the Great Hall were a great inspiration to people who heard him in person or distantly from the playing fields below. Richard Knight, the admissions tutor, was a skilled oboe player, a rare enough talent at the time. Colin Gough was and is a marvellous violin player and has appeared on many editions of the British Broadcasting Corporation's third programme, both on his own and in a consort of viols, that was a regular programme for quite some time. Kenneth McFadyen was two-thirds physicist and one-third musician and developed an instrument for producing 'musique concrete', an electronic version of a pianoforte instrumental keyboard. Philip Moon, as head of the department, was an accomplished pianist. I remember having dinner with Winifred and Philip Moon on our arrival at Birmingham when he played the piano and I sang some of the lieder songs of years ago in this somewhat impromptu concert setting. This experience forged a sort of bond that made me a small part of the musical culture of the department.

The University of Manitoba also has an active musical presence in the physics department. Tom Osborn, a theoretical physicist, and his wife, Patricia Spencer, a flautist, played a major role in the promotion and performance (respectively) of the group called the Aurora Musicale which existed for more than a decade in Winnipeg. Other members of the department play various instruments. John Page plays the violin, and his wife, Shelley, the harpsichord with great accomplishment. Juris Svenne participates in the Winnipeg Opera Company and sings both solo and chorally, as and when required by the physics department.

Others participate in organisational or listening roles and are fascinated by both classical and modern music. Indeed, if music is the food of physics, may we all continue to be sustained.

Chapter Seventeen

The Physicist Has Problems with Air, Fire and Water

The non-stop flight from Shannon airport to London Heathrow is normally a comfortable and delightful experience. The charm, efficiency and soft speech of the Aer Lingus cabin staff serve to make the experience a memorable one. So much service, so little time to enjoy it!

On one occasion, however, in the late Seventies, the physicist was returning by air from a visit to University College, Galway. The time was late September, and the plane was massively underbooked. I sat in an aisle seat on the left-hand side of the aircraft, a Boeing 737. Just prior to departure both seats to my left remained empty. At virtually the last minute before leaving, I became aware that a late arrival was clambering across my feet towards the window seat, carrying a substantial wooden box. He settled momentarily into his seat, only to then alternately stand up and sit down. On taking off, he appeared composed, but on reaching cruising altitude at thirty thousand feet, he recommenced his agitated activity and retrieved articles from his box with which he generated loud knocking sounds. I sat motionless, pretending to read the *New Scientist*, but in reality wondering what he would do next. It therefore came as no surprise when the fellow leaned across and tapped me on the shoulder. 'I wonder if you can help me,' he said. 'I don't seem to be able to open the window!' Now, attempting to open a sealed window on a jet airliner at thirty thousand feet is clearly an unhappy practice that must be discouraged at all costs. My horror at his suggestion must have been evident from my facial expression, but he, poor fellow, was totally unaware of the enormity of his request. It took the entire hour of flying time and a great deal of patience to explain to him that jet aircraft are pressurised and that had his mission proved successful it would likely have ended the flying careers of many of the passengers including himself. The explanation of his behaviour was however in the end to some sense understandable. He had left his native home in Bombay, India, several years previously and had travelled overland and by sea to Ireland. The employment he obtained there was steady and well paying, and finally he had saved up sufficient funds for a triumphant return home by air – his first flight.

Since that time, on each flight I listen carefully to the cabin staff outlining safety instructions to all passengers. No one can be in any doubt as to how to buckle or unbuckle a safety belt, where the emergency exits are located or where the lighted path to an exit is to be found. Never, however, have I heard the instruction, 'On no account attempt to open the windows on this aircraft.' The fact that there are people out there who may seek to do so is frightening in the extreme. Perhaps a suitable amendment to IATA safety instructions might prove both beneficial and reassuring to all concerned with safety in international air travel.

★

Many years previously and shortly after his arrival in Birmingham the physicist found himself working in a small office located directly above the site of the Radial Ridge cyclotron facility, and a short distance from a small conference room. The view from his desk was of green grass falling away towards the Bristol Road and the university playing fields. The only visual feature of interest was a door located on a chariot-like device which appeared to be an entrance into the hill proper. Whether it was a storage area for maintenance equipment or served some quite different purpose I neither knew nor cared. It was simply a part of my immediate visual environment.

One Saturday afternoon in late spring, the physicist was working at his lecture preparation for the following week, when an unusual sight drew itself to his attention. It was a small plume of smoke hanging above the doorway into the hillside. As he watched, the density of smoke increased in intensity and fingers of the soot-like emission wreathed themselves around all sides of the entrance. Fire! I thought and immediately leapt to my feet. I dashed outside with a purpose worthy of young Lochinvar. Being alone in the building clearly only my own actions could save the day. I hastened to the door, pulled hard on the handles and rolled back the trolley on which the door stood.

Immediately a dense cloud of smoke emptied, darkening the sky all around the hill. Further smoke continued to belch out of the hole as if from a subterranean furnace. I ran rapidly back to an emergency telephone inside the laboratory. While making the call I noticed that the smoke had started to clear somewhat and to my amazement teams of miners in firefighting gear emerged only to stand huddled in the bright sunlight.

It was at this precise moment that the truth came to light and the enormity of my actions became apparent. The voice on the other end of the emergency telephone explained everything in simple terms. Apparently the University of Birmingham with its great science and engineering heritage boasted a department of mining, the only one left in the country. This department possessed an experimental mine with a small shaft and galleries built into the hill beside the physics department.

The particular Saturday on which I sprang into action was the culmination of a National Mine Safety Week. Teams of firefighters from collieries throughout Britain were competing for a trophy of some kind, and finding their way through smoke-filled corridors to fame and success – at least until miraculously the smoke cleared and the competition was abandoned. Once the truth was known, there was little that the physicist could say or do. Far from exhibiting further heroics, discretion suddenly appeared to be the better part of valour. In any case, a milling crowd of very fit, very large miners, determined to disembody the opener of the door, did little to encourage academic conversation. At 5 p.m. precisely I left by the door farthest from the scene of the incident. My wife was delighted to see me home so early for a change.

The department of mining was closed some time later; no connection of course.

*

Few outdoor activities or sports can compare with fishing as a wholesome source of relaxation for the troubled physicist. The tranquillity, inactivity, and timelessness of lake and river angling contrast sharply with the frantic, round-the-clock, mental and physical exercise encountered on a daily basis by the practising research scientist. Standing for hours on a pier in pouring rain and catching nothing but pneumonia may seem a masochistic waste of time. However, the mere fact of being outside in the open air and not financially dependent upon catching fish for supper provide a degree of equanimity seldom matched and never surpassed. Such delights should be shared, and who better to encourage in the sport than one's children, specifically in the case of the physicist, his son.

One summer, with my boy, Conor, approaching his tenth birthday, I decided to buy him a fishing rod. It was of good quality, with a fine reel and a stout line capable of playing a whale. We were on holiday on the west coast of Ireland, enjoying exceptional weather and some boredom. As a result, after a fine morning on the beautiful beach at Gorteen, two miles from the fishing port of Roundstone, Conor and I decided to leave mother and young sister to their own devices and go in search of *le joli poisson* as the French tourists describe the silver darlings.

We wandered along the rocks by the shoreline in the general direction of Roundstone, and came across a little natural harbour, a cleft between two black basalt outcrops, where the water was deep and clear, and there was no other human being as far as the eye could see. On the right-hand side of the harbour was a flat shelf of rock from which casting a line should be a piece of cake. My son began to attempt casting his line, and succeeded in snaring both his socks and his dad. Eager to act as instructor, despite a notable lack of angling skill, I then commandeered the rod and demonstrated how the line should be held firmly against the rod as it was swung forward and then released when it had acquired its maximum forward speed. My demonstration was not impressive. Indeed, I forgot to release my finger grip at the correct moment and as a result the hook almost caught my sandal which was firmly planted on dry land.

'Let me do it!' said Conor.

'No. Just watch me carefully this time. Then, you can do the same!' said I.

Conor watched impatiently as I extended my arm backwards prior to casting. This time I gave the rod a really good forward swing and released the hold of my fingers on the line. Unfortunately, however, I omitted to continue to hold the rod. As a result, the fishing rod described an elegant arc and travelled ten feet horizontally before sinking effortlessly into twelve feet of clear sea water. There was one moment of unbearable silence before my son, with understandable anguish, broke into howls of disappointment and disbelief. How could his father have performed this dastardly deed and thrown away the present he had only recently been given.

'Try to be quiet and let your father think,' said the physicist.

Conor was not to be comforted, so reluctantly and in some embarrassment he was returned to the rest of the family at Gorteen, while his father contemplated his options for recovery of the rod.

I was never a great swimmer. I had learned the breaststroke and a bastardised form of sidestroke, but was limited in performance of both. Lessons in diving from a three-metre board at Portrush harbour had resulted in limited proficiency at this art. For these reasons, diving into twelve feet of water and recovering the missing rod might present some difficulty. There being no one around the little harbour but myself, I quickly stripped down to my undershorts and dived heroically into the cold water. Many times I repeated the attempt but basic incompetence coupled with poor eyesight ensured that this exercise would end in failure. Never did I reach within a metre of the clearly visible object.

I sat down on a rock and contemplated the situation. As I did so, I suddenly noticed a farmer in a field nearby, a quarter of a mile or so away, who was building a haycock or haystack, it being haymaking time. This he did by means of a pitchfork with an ultra-long handle. The idea then came to mind that here was the solution to my problem. I would borrow the pitchfork and dive down with the forked end outstretched before me. I would snare the fishing rod, come to the surface and swim triumphantly to shore.

Borrowing the pitchfork was simple. The farmer was ready for his tea; I promised to return the fork in half an hour and off I went. Failure again dogged my rescue efforts. The pitchfork was of course of metal origin, but it had a wooden sleeve around the handle. In water, the buoyancy of the wood equalled the weight of iron or steel. As a result, my dives were even more shallow than before, and this time the equipment hardly broke the surface of the water. I sat down to think again. The solution dawned on me suddenly! What I had to do was to hold my breath for an extended period, climb down the face of the rock shelf on which I stood, until I reached the bottom, then crawl along the harbour floor for ten feet to the rod, place the pitchfork under the handle and reel and then allow the trio of fork, rod and attached physicist to rise confidently to the surface.

I remembered that at high school I had once won the 'hold your breath' contest with a time of around two minutes. I did not however appreciate the work I would have to do in forcing the buoyant pitchfork down the underwater cliff and the energy I would expend in holding it against the buoyant force while on the bottom. After several fruitless attempts, I resolved to make a final determined effort. I sat for some time, clad only in my boxer shorts, practised holding my breath for as long as possible and then descended rapidly down the rock face. At the bottom, lying heavily on top of the pitchfork and directing it purposefully towards the rod, I kicked off from the side without attempting to crawl along the bottom. Needless to say, the fork again missed the rod by at least a metre, and shot upward like an arrow to the surface where the sputtering physicist suddenly appeared, trident in hand, like some denizen rising from the deep. What followed is not only unbelievable, but true. The rocky harbour that had been devoid of human presence was now transformed. Some thirty or so persons with cameras, binoculars and the like were assembled on top of the west bank of the little inlet in what was clearly an ornithologists' day outing. All eyes were on the physicist, and it took him little time to assess the situation. I swam as quickly as I could with the pitchfork to the bank from which this sorry affair had started. Grabbing my clothes, I ran quickly away and back to the safe confines of Gorteen beach, stopping only briefly to return to the farmer his useless aid in my endeavours.

I have often wondered since then what the birdwatchers thought they had seen back at the harbour. Was it a rare sighting of 'the lesser panted McKee' or a manifestation of King Neptune exhibiting his displeasure to his subjects? We will never know. What is straightforward is the finale to this tale. At supper that evening, in the Seal's Rock Hotel, the young fourteen year old son of a well known Dublin judge learned of Conor's great misfortune. Being a young dolphin himself and rarely either out of the sea or without his flippers, he asked if I would drive him to the scene of the incident and show him the problem. On arrival, he dove straight into the water and in one simple movement brought the fine fishing rod to the surface. I thanked him, looked around at the now totally empty landscape and decided that fishing was far too much fun for mere mortals to enjoy.

I wonder if I should have taught Conor to play bridge.

Chapter Eighteen

The Physicist Aspires to Political Office

'All in the April evening, April airs were abroad', or so the old song goes.

Herein may lie the only explanation of my strange behaviour one spring night. It must have been the air. How else can one account for an otherwise sound and single-minded research physicist agreeing to run for election to the provincial legislature in Manitoba.

Circumstances certainly were unusual in the spring of 1988. The incumbent New Democratic government had fallen as a result of the somewhat eccentric behaviour of the speaker in voting against his own party. An election was called and the Liberal Party was hurriedly nominating candidates for all seats in the province. Things looked simple in the Tuxedo constituency of Winnipeg City. Here an intelligent and able candidate already existed in Jim Carr. He was not only popular but had contested the seat in the previous election in 1985, and was in every sense a favourite son of both party and riding.

The meeting of Tuxedo Liberal Party Executives was called with a single purpose, namely to arrange a venue and date for Jim Carr's nomination meeting. The Executive Committee comprised a number of prominent Liberals. Campbell Wright, whose father had run for office in the area some years previously, was chair, and incidentally a lawyer. Mark O'Neill was another bright young lawyer, George Sisler was a leading psychiatrist. My wife, Christine, and I were also members. Roy Lev was an architect. As the meeting was about to begin, a bombshell was dropped. A message from Jim indicated that he had decided to seek nomination in the Osborn riding rather than in Tuxedo. His decision while understandable was nonetheless totally unexpected. He was moving to more traditional Liberal territory, and had been wooed by the local election committee. The facts then were simple. The writ for the election had been dropped, and Tuxedo constituency was without a Liberal candidate, or even the prospect of one.

At the meeting, all was consternation until someone said, 'The situation is clear: one of us must run.' Everyone looked at each other in an atmosphere of confusion if not panic.

'It will have to be Jasper,' said a voice.

'How about it?' asked the chair, Campbell Wright.

I looked at Christine, and she looked back at me. 'Oh, why not?' she said, and suddenly the die was cast. Previously in my academic career I would not have even considered running for political office. It would have been the death knell for a promising career in physics. Leave scientific research for even half a year and you lose sight of the frontier you pursue and will never recover. Many times, while in Birmingham, I had been asked to run for city council as a Liberal, but had never given the opportunity more than passing thought. Physics was too exciting for such a distraction, and so any support I gave was from afar. However the challenge before me was suddenly a more interesting one. Few politicians seemed to appreciate the importance of science to the community and Canada. Funding for research was beginning to disappear. Research and development carried out by industry was dismally inadequate, and good students were beginning to look elsewhere for scientific careers and fulfilment. Some scientists would have to become political even if they were in no sense 'political scientists'. As an established academic and a past president of the Canadian Association of Physicists it suddenly dawned on me that now might be the time to make an excursion into the political arena. So I did.

The nomination meeting at Shaftesbury High School was well attended and I was duly nominated. Campbell Wright and David Walker, later to become the Member of Parliament for Winnipeg North, jointly managed my campaign. I was tightly controlled, not even attending campaign strategy meetings. I went door-to-door, morning, noon and night, from start to finish of the campaign. However almost two weeks into the campaign my dear mother died suddenly in a nursing home in Northern Ireland, in her ninetieth year. She had been ill for some time but her death was a tragic shock. I left the campaign to others for eight days, after which I returned with renewed vigour and determination.

Up to this point I have not mentioned the fact that my opponent in Tuxedo was Gary Filmon, the newly-elected leader of the Conservative Party. Should his party win the election then he would become Premier of the province. His career had been considerable in the political arena, both as a long-term city councillor and then as a member of the legislature. He had not however been overly visible for some time in his Tuxedo constituency. Going door-to-door early in the election campaign, an elderly woman asked me at the door, who was my Conservative opponent? I told her that it was Gary Filmon. 'Oh no, young man,' she said (I liked the 'young'), 'we used to have a city councillor of that name, but I think he retired.' So, the stage was set for battle. The local Liberal team was fantastic. We had volunteers coming out of our ears, and the candidate was never without company at any door, and often teams of four or five went out together. The poll organisation under Jan Jardine and Wayne Oncholenko was excellent and almost every area in the large riding was covered effectively.

Two problems existed however that were eventually to prove crucial. Firstly, the advanced polls involving residents who would be out of town on election day, turned out to be overwhelmingly for Filmon. My late nomination and lack of early visibility affected those polls as no others. Also, a new residential subdivision had grown up in the south of the constituency in an area known as Lindenwoods. This population had gone from a few hundred to almost two thousand in three years, and a local in-area committee was left to blanket the district as an almost separate campaign. After visiting homes in the area early in the campaign, canvassing there was left to the local group. This strategy turned out to be the Achilles heel of the Liberal election plan in Tuxedo. As an upscale area, it required concentrated and particular attention.

As election day approached, an air of excitement and anticipation entered the campaign. Workers became buoyed up by responses at the doors, and it became increasingly clear that the impossible might become reality and we could win. Tales of the challenges encountered late in the election are many. Conservatives were attempting to inveigle me into their homes to discuss policy items at length and thereby get me off the streets. My handlers however were unyielding in their refusal to lose sight of me even for a moment. The contrasts in method between the Conservatives and the Liberals were marked. Signs for the Tories were mounted on steel poles by professional paid workers. For the Liberals, all signs were on wooden stakes and mounted by a volunteer team led by my son, Conor. Conor carried signs and poles around in the old battered family Chevrolet Malibu, or his own even more battered Buick. He did not wait for orders. He decided where a sign would be visible, noticeable and effective, and then approached the appropriate homeowner for permission to mount a McKee sign. Often the owners of the sites were politically undecided, so Conor would undertake to guarantee a personal visit from the candidate in exchange for mounting the highly visible sign. The sign war was clearly won by the amateurs.

Anecdotal tales abound after elections are won and lost. Late in the campaign, two colleagues and I were going house-to-house on a road south of Corydon Street. At the front door stood a notice saying to any callers, 'Go to the back door.' We dutifully obliged. However, passing down the side of the house, it was necessary to pass the most vicious-looking beast I have ever seen. Black in colour and resembling a huge German Shepherd, teeth bared and straining on a chain link leash, it left a space of about one foot between teeth and wall, with leash fully extended. One by one with backs pressed to the wall we slipped past the Baskervillian hound and arrived at the back door. Here we found another notice, similar to that observed earlier, which said simply, 'Go to the front door.' Seeking election is never easy. The people not only speak, but occasionally make democracy a dangerous pastime.

Eventually, on the night before election day, teams of Liberal canvassers were out all over the constituency, having a last visit with the undecided. It was like a love-in! People came out of their houses to wish us luck, and when two supporters and I went door-to-door around Mathers Bay area, we could find no one who was left undecided. At that moment, Liberal was the thing to be. After an hour or so of euphoric responses, Mark O'Neill, a young lawyer working with me, and literally running from house to house said loudly, 'This is great; it certainly beats sex.'

And so we came to election day. It is not relevant or appropriate in a vignette of this kind to discuss the platform on which I ran, or the policies of the provincial Liberal and Conservative parties. In a nutshell, I have always adopted a marginally left of centre approach to politics, being on the one side a strong supporter of small business as the engine of the provincial economy, while believing deeply in the necessity for a continually caring society. So, election day arrived.

The weather on the big day was warm and fair. Christine and I voted early and later on I visited many of the polling stations in the riding. David Walker kept me moving while we visited several places, co-operative housing areas and the like, hoping to encourage unlikely voters to take the plunge and 'just do it'.

When the polls closed, Campbell Wright, my other co-manager, joined me at home with a bottle of Moët et Chandon champagne as fortification. It was not long after eight o'clock when the first result came in. It was a poll at the Canadian forces base that returned only three votes, two for McKee and one for Filmon. The cheers at headquarters could almost be heard at the house, according to observers of the scene.

Further results came in, then more, until by the time most had been declared, I was still leading in Tuxedo with not too many polls still to report. Those still unaccounted for however included advanced polls and Lindenwoods.

When Campbell and I left for the campaign office at around 9.30 p.m. the situation was still unclear. Indeed, it was on the journey to the office that the lead finally changed to Filmon and in the end stayed that way. On arrival we were met by television cameras and the usual raft of reporters who smell an upset in the making. I recall making a 'sort-of' acceptance speech to Marjorie Salki of CKY TV just prior to learning that the late polls were shifting the balance inexorably to Gary Filmon. By 10.30 p.m. it seemed that the cause was lost by one hundred and thirty votes. Later a mobile hospital polling station reported six more votes for McKee leaving the final result as a Conservative win by one hundred and twenty-four votes. Almost all that remained was to thank an incredible team of workers and supporters, a team that had both fought the good fight and had fun while doing it.

There was however one more important matter to address, namely congratulating the winner, soon to become Premier, on his victory. He was supposed to be celebrating at Rumours Comedy Club, but because of the uncertainties of the evening and the lateness of the hour he could not be found. I eventually was convinced by my escorts to give up and leave it until morning.

The question of a recount was also being raised but that would be addressed in the fullness of time.

The following morning, having continued to fail miserably in my efforts to contact Gary Filmon even at his home, I wrote what I hoped was an appropriately gracious letter and determined to deliver it by hand to his home in Jaymoor. A simple enough task, one would think. The driveway to the Filmon home has a loop in it that enables a car to drive up to the door, drop off people or things and then continue around and out by the entrance route. On my arrival, life was not quite as simple as that would suggest. A truck filled with election signs was parked halfway round the 'in' part of the loop, so I was obliged to park behind this obstacle and walk across the lawn to the front door to deliver my missive. I rang the bell several times before a bleary-eyed and, I suspect, hungover offspring of the Filmon clan answered the call. I explained my mission, he received the note, withdrew and closed the door. Now all I needed to do was return home and report the result of my visit. This is where things got out of hand.

The driveway was not overly wide, and because of the parked truck I was obliged to reverse out of the driveway. Now, just at the spot where the entrance road and loop meet stood the Filmon mailbox. When I say it stood there, it would be more accurate to say that it hung there. The overall supporting structure was that of a medieval 'gibbet'. An arm projected towards the driveway, and the mailbox was suspended from the end of this arm for easy access. Unfortunately, I had not taken note of either mailbox or gibbet. From my driving mirror all I saw as I reversed was tightly-cropped green lawn and the surface of the roadway. Driving confidently backward I however managed to strike the end of the gibbet-arm thus fracturing the structure and depositing the mailbox and contents on the lawn. The mail had clearly been accumulating for a day or two, and was now broadcast evenly over a small section of grass. I exited the car and surveyed the still life exhibit that I had created.

Some minutes later, I again approached the front door of the Filmon residence. I rang the bell. There was a pause. Then the same young man, still looking like a tree full of owls, emerged blinking into the sunlight. I mumbled something about being sorry to have destroyed his mailbox and asked him to tell his father to have it repaired and send the bill directly to me. He seemed to indicate that he would do so. The bill however was never to arrive. Instead, I received, some weeks later, a copy of a Snoopy cartoon in which the little chap was leaping up and down on a similar mailbox and destroying it efficiently. The bubble above his head with the three words STOMP, STOMP, STOMP, seemed to indicate the satisfaction available from such villainy. May all politicians develop a sense of humour to protect them from the excesses of their political opponents.

Returning to the result of the election, and the political situation created, Filmon was now Premier of the Province of Manitoba and his party held a slim five member majority over the Liberals in a minority government.

The Tuxedo result, had it been reversed would have resulted in the defeat of the Premier and a high degree of political instability. For this reason alone, the advice from my legal advisers was not to contest the final result. A recount we felt was unlikely to change the final numbers substantially as Liberal scrutineers had been active at virtually every polling station.

What was of more concern was the very first poll that reported, the one where only three votes were recorded. Returns from the Canadian forces base were in general favourable to Liberal candidates, and each poll should have embraced a couple of hundred votes. The question as to why only three votes were counted in that one poll has never been answered. There was no sudden exodus of personnel on active service and there appeared to be a normal voters' list available for that poll. The question could only be addressed by a judicial enquiry, and the matter would take months to complete. The advice I received was 'forget it'. Whatever the result might have been, the political scene could do without such continuing uncertainty.

So ended the story of Tuxedo, 1988. As a footnote, the boundaries of Tuxedo constituency were altered dramatically by the time the 1990 election came around. By then, Jasper McKee, without changing his address was a resident of River Heights and no longer of Tuxedo. The changing face of politics is difficult for the average voter to deal with or understand. For the politician it may be impossible.

Chapter Nineteen

The Physicist as a Scientific Communicator

A successful educator has always had vision, enthusiasm, knowledge and the ability to communicate effectively with students. Teaching has always been a challenging career but never more so than at the present time. A constantly changing curriculum, social problems among students, disciplinary problems within and without the classroom, and the scarcity of job opportunities all combine to make a difficult task more demanding than before.

There is a story told of a woman in Winnipeg who called her son at seven thirty in the morning, shouting, 'Jimmy, get up and have your breakfast otherwise you'll be late for school!'

'I'm not going to school today,' said Jimmy. 'I don't feel like it. None of the kids like me; none of the teachers like me; even the janitors don't talk to me. I'm not getting up. I'm not going to school.'

'But you have to, Jimmy,' said his mother. 'Remember you are almost forty years old and you're the Principal!'

This tale perhaps overemphasises the stresses placed on the educator at the present time. But then, on the other hand, perhaps not.

This chapter will not address, in any way, teaching of the curriculum to students at junior or high school. It involves the communication of scientific knowledge to laypeople who may need it or who believe they require it. The questions discussed can be chosen by an educator, by a student, or by any layperson. The means of communication may be through personal contact, through public lecture, radio, or television. The solution in each case will depend on the specific nature of the problem to be addressed and the minimum amount of new knowledge that needs to be transferred.

I recall, in the late 1960s, a science reporter with the British Broadcasting Corporation stating categorically that water flowing through a plughole would flow in a different direction in the northern and southern hemispheres because of a strange phenomenon known as the Coriolis force. For dramatic effect, the spokesperson stated that if you were in a ship sailing across the equator from north to south and letting the water out of your bath at the time, you would be astonished to find the water stops flowing in an anticlockwise direction and changes to a clockwise direction as the equator was crossed. This, of course, is transparent nonsense. The Coriolis force, which arises from the inadequacy of Newton's Laws of Motion in dealing with rotating systems, while having several visible manifestations in the natural world is very difficult to demonstrate in this particular situation. Indeed, if you take a vessel filled with water, it will be some forty hours before all oscillation of the water resulting from the filling process will have disappeared. In addition, the process by which a plug is pulled out of a bath often determines the direction in which the water will flow. So the same bath may produce widely differing results dependent upon the method by which the plug is removed. A bath with an electrically-operated shutter as a plug is therefore necessary to ensure that the removal of the plug does not have a greater effect on the water and its flow than anything else. It is also clear that the shape of the vessel is of overriding importance. A symmetrical vessel with a central exit hole is ideal for this demonstration!

The purpose of this detailed account of the difficulties of demonstrating proper direction of rotation of flowing water is to understand the problem encountered by a maker of baths at Darlaston in England. He attempted to confirm the lesson he had just learned from BBC radio by filling all twenty of a set of identical baths, approximately eight feet long and three feet wide, to the same level and then simultaneously removing all the plugs and recording the direction of flow of the water. Needless to say, the flow was in the opposite direction to that identified by the broadcaster for the simple reason that, of the factors involved, the overriding one was the shape of the bath. The plug hole in these baths was situated at one end underneath the taps, and the flow of water from the rest of the bath to the plughole was dominated by geometry rather than esoteric physics.

I recall a story told to me once about two teachers who took a day's vacation in the autumn and decided to do something they had never done before, namely, go duck hunting. So they met in the early morning, taking their dogs with them, and spent twelve hours engaged in this new sport. At dusk they had not a single duck to show for their efforts and collapsed exhausted in a local hostelry where they each drank a pint of beer and sat disconsolately looking at each other. Eventually one of them said to the other, 'I'm sure we must be doing something terribly wrong.' Shortly afterwards the other one acknowledged that this might well be the case. Then, some twenty minutes later, the first one suddenly looked up and said, 'I know what it is. We aren't throwing the dogs up high enough.'

The problem with duck hunting, as with science, is that inadequate knowledge can lead you in entirely the wrong direction. This was certainly true of the Darlaston factory owner and is clearly the fault of the simplistic broadcaster who was trying to enlighten the public.

My first self-generated contact with the public-at-large took place in 1971 on my return from a nuclear physics conference held in Liverpool University in the spring of that year. On arrival at Lime Street Station in Liverpool, my attention had been drawn to several hundred British troops assembled on the platform prior to embarkation for Northern Ireland. This was, of course, in the early days of the renewed 'troubles' as they're called. These troops were clad in combat dress, a green and brown uniform conspicuously unsuitable for military service in a hostile, grey and concrete environment such as Belfast or Londonderry. I knew that colours such as red and green are seldom seen in modern downtown urban surroundings. Greys and browns tend to predominate. For this reason, a green or red post box or automobile is clearly distinguishable, even at a distance, as a matter of contrast rather than of luminosity and the same should be true of a green uniform. Another factor relevant to this observation is the Purkinje effect, which I had studied in an experimental psychology course as a physics undergraduate. It is rather easy to show that, as the intensity of visible light decreases, so the region of maximum sensitivity of the eye shifts from yellow to green. The fact that grass looks greenest at sundown is a manifestation of this phenomenon. It seemed to me, therefore, that a green uniform, at dusk, in a concrete environment would become a highly conspicuous object. I felt, warming to this theme, that a reform of military uniform was perhaps overdue for soldiers engaged in urban guerrilla conflict and, in a letter to *The Times*, I suggested that perhaps storm trooper grey or khaki battle dress would be, on the face of it, more suitable than the currently accepted alternatives. I had never previously written a letter to *The Times* but understood that, if you had a point to make and it seemed important enough to you, then you would leave it to the editors of *The Times* to determine whether publication was appropriate or not.

Now the trouble with my action was not that my observations were essentially incorrect or that the matter was not of great interest to a wider public. It was that all hell broke loose on the publication of the letter. Firstly, one or two tabloid newspapers took up the story and splashed it on the front page. Then, there was the inevitable question in the House of Commons and a response from the Secretary of Defence culminating with a series of radio interviews from the BBC broadcasting studios at Pebble Mill Road in which many questions, some scientific and some not, were asked, including 'Was I in any danger as a result of my observation?' This question did little to delight my family and friends who knew of my nativity in one of the cities under discussion. Becoming an overnight expert in the field of urban battle dress had never been my intention. The fact that a simple scientific observation had generated such a furore did little for either my daily lecturing routine or my equanimity. This exercise in communication was, however, very instructive. It taught me, above all things, to think things through to a logical conclusion rather than be carried away by the initial solution.

This is not unlike the situation encountered by a young teacher who had arrived in Manitoba and discovered that he had a natural talent for growing pumpkins. He bought a piece of land at the junction between a provincial highway and a municipal road and found that as harvest time approached, his pumpkins were becoming the talk of the town. But as they grew bigger and bigger, he found that one or two of them started to go missing and it became imperative that he find a quick solution to the problem. Being an intelligent chap, he did not have to think for long. He established a notice board at the junction of the two roads and illuminated it with bright fluorescent lighting and placed upon it the important piece of information which stated, 'Beware, one of these pumpkins is poisoned!' A week or so later, when he went to inspect his pumpkin farm, he was delighted to find that, as far as he could tell, every single one of his champions was still there and, much relieved, he decided to go home for supper. But as he passed the notice board at the junction of the roads, it seemed to him that everything was not identically the same as it had been before. When he went up to the notice board, he discovered the change. The notice read 'Now two of the pumpkins are poisoned.' So, in all walks of life it is important to distinguish between an initial and a final solution to a problem. Even in communicating science, it is important to think things through.

Now, for those of you who have never had the need or perhaps the opportunity to appear on radio or television as a communicator of science to the public, it might be instructive if I run briefly through my history as a science broadcaster in Canada. It all began around Christmas 1979. The Faculty of Science had decided to launch a magic show for school kids. It was free and it was varied and students were bussed in from various schools in and around the city. The local CBC radio station heard about the project and wished for someone to come and discuss its success or otherwise on air at seven forty on the following Monday morning. It was never originally intended that I would play any part in this interview but the person selected was heroically reluctant to participate and, at the last minute, the Dean's office got in touch with me as a participant in this extravaganza and asked if I would fill the breach. Part of my act, which was popular at the time, was to freeze a banana with liquid nitrogen and then beat nails into a large piece of balsa wood, using it as a hammer. For my early morning show on Monday it was therefore necessary for me to take to the studio, not only myself and the other equipment, but both a small and a large dewar of liquid nitrogen – the large one being necessary to refill the small one as many times as were required for the show. On leaving my home at 7 a.m. on Monday, my daughter, Siobhan, asked in a concerned manner whether I was really sure that this was radio and not television because she could not herself see the point in taking all this equipment into a studio from which nothing but sound would emanate. So, with a carload of equipment and in a cloud of doubt, I left for the studio. In the end, all went well. I gave my demonstrations and when a repeat was called for I replenished the small dewar with liquid nitrogen from the large one, pouring excess nitrogen all over the studio table and causing the host, now the member of parliament for St James in Winnipeg, John Harvard, to leap in the air and throw over his chair with dramatic effect. Some days after this event, I got a telephone call at the physics department from the producer saying that the Monday morning programme had been unusually well received and they were wondering whether, on a semi-regular basis, I might come in and discuss an item of scientific news with them, which I agreed to do. The programme soon became weekly.

The initial interview with my producer was particularly helpful. It was made clear to me that this was news and was not a lecture. There was no suggestion that I would gradually and logically work up to a punch line or coda at the end of my presentation. The scientific result, the exciting news item, had to be up front and covered within the first sentence of the interview. This gave the listener no chance to switch radio channels prior to being informed. It was also pointed out that I must quickly get a feeling for a period of five or six minutes, the actual time depending on the local situation on a particular day. When the host or hostess would start waving the right hand in circular motion, that meant I was to wind up directly, not in a few minutes, but immediately if not sooner. I had my own 'stinger', which is a piece of music to indicate that a certain programme is about to follow. I do not now recall the music involved but 'stingers' became passé after the first five years or so. Being a question and answer format, it was always important not to get too bogged down in the answers to early questions, in case the thrust of the interview was lost in wind-up procedures.

Initially, each five or six minutes piece was discussed at length with the producer, and perhaps the host, in advance of the production. But, after a few years, I would get to the studio at the last minute, be handed a little piece of paper with the selected questions on it, and attempt to handle whatever transpired.

During the nine years of this show, a host of hosts and hostesses came and went. John Harvard was translated to higher things, eventually becoming a Member of Parliament, Agatha Moir took over from him, to be followed by Bill Guest, Tom McCullough, Sandy Coleman on occasion, Leslie Hughes, Doug McIlraith and others that are almost too numerous to mention. My appearances were so regular, at seven forty on a Tuesday morning, that people began to assume that I was there even when I was not. I would slip into the studio as my 'stinger' was playing, the programme would take place, and off I would go. On one occasion, stuck firmly in snow and ice on the Maryland bridge and some ten or fifteen minutes by foot from the studio, I heard it announced confidently that I had just entered the studio and would be appearing within a few moments. At this point, I left my car, put the hood up, and fought my way through the snow to enter the studio as the 'stinger' finished, and as my interview was about to start

Apparently nobody had noticed my absence, from producer downwards.

Towards the end of my stint with the *Morning Show*, there was a system in place that had dual hosts. One was Leslie Hughes, who had served as single host for some time, and the other was Doug McIlraith, an excellent storyteller as well as interviewer. When this redoubtable duo was involved, one of them would read the introduction to the interview, give the background, and perhaps ask the first question, then leave the studio for coffee while the second would interact freely with the interviewee and ask the remaining questions. On one particular occasion, Doug McIlraith read the introduction and gave the background but did not ask the first question. Leslie Hughes asked the first question and then immediately left to call her children to make sure they were awake and ready for school. Doug had already gone to replenish his coffee cup. The producer was interviewing a small musical group outside the studio in preparation for the following hour, with the result that for something like five minutes I was left to talk to myself, asking rhetorical questions and then answering them to the best of my ability. Only the technician, John Robertson remained.

I have often thought since that time that if this had been my first appearance on the air, I would probably never have agreed to repeat it. But having once played Macbeth at school when Banquo forgot all his lines and seemed unable to hear the prompter, ad libbing was an art to which I had already subscribed and all was not lost.

In 1988, I was persuaded to make a little excursion into the political arena and, as a result, became politically unclean and had to terminate my regular CBC morning spot. However, as it so happened, once the election was over and *Newsworld*, the television programme, had been born and had a two-hour spot from Winnipeg, I became a scientific columnist and had a regular Friday lunchtime spot with either Ann Petrie or Bob Sideiko. Television is a more difficult medium than radio and it is often important to put the essence of what you want to say in a twelve or fifteen second clip. On *Newsworld*, however, in the early days, time was not of the essence and I was involved in five-minute episodes similar to those previously broadcast on radio. Now, however, there was the additional problem of getting made up before going on air and, hopefully, getting the makeup removed before returning to the university for afternoon class. This was something that I often forgot. In addition, if a television interview was pre-recorded, it might never be aired for reasons that would not have existed in a radio programme. I remember, for example, that a particularly lively and, I thought, interesting discussion on remote sensing was never aired because the broadcast timed for the following day was bumped by a report from a Premiers' conference. As the date of our recording was just prior to Remembrance Day, both the hostess and I were wearing poppies, and the moment for transmission was suddenly gone. The programme could not be broadcast later because of the poppies.

While working with *Newsworld* I learned how to produce efficient three-minute commentaries on controversial matters and to use the rolling screen mechanism in which the lines on the television screen move upwards at a rate controlled directly by the speed of my speech. I also took part in several coast-to-coast phone-in shows which are an art form in themselves. Usually there would be one person being interviewed in Toronto or elsewhere while I was being interviewed in Winnipeg. Both of us, on a split screen, would be seen simultaneously by the viewer and both would be responding to the same question from any listener who cared to phone in.

During one of these one-hour programmes, technicians controlling the balance between the two halves of the screen, the one showing my opponent and the other showing me, observed that my picture was becoming somewhat cloudy and much less clear than that of the interviewee in Toronto. I also became aware of a great deal of activity around my feet which were firmly planted under the studio table. Being summer, although I was respectably clad from the waist up, I was wearing boat shoes on my feet, which had a low-grade plastic sole. My right foot was firmly ensconced upon a cold light set in the floor but, apparently, the heat from the light bulb was still sufficient to melt the plastic and seal my foot firmly to the floor. Indeed, it was vapour from molten plastic arising round the table that was clouding the picture of the physicist in Winnipeg, as yet blissfully unaware of the chaos around and below him. A message in my earplug, suggesting that I continue as if nothing had happened, did little to comfort me as up to that time I had not been aware of anything untoward occurring. Finally, two technicians working in concert managed, with adequate strength, to tear my molten sole from the floor to which it had been welded. No one at the television studio could ever recall such an incident occurring previously. Having proceeded throughout the programme as if nothing unusual was afoot gave me some local notoriety in the weeks and months which followed.

By 1990, however, there was another change in television programming and *Newsworld* was transferred to Calgary for operating purposes and Ann Petrie went with it. At this point, I was approached by the producer of the afternoon CBC radio show from Winnipeg with an idea for a quite different science programme. The idea here was that I would not generate news or other scientific items but would respond to questions raised by the public at large, questions relating to their observation of the world around them but confined to problems in the physical sciences. It was not clear, initially, whether there would be many questions forthcoming from the public nor that they would be of any wide interest.

However, some five years later when the last of these programmes took place, there was still a backlog of questions to be answered and every indication of a thirst for scientific knowledge in the public at large.

The success of the programme is reviewed in the following chapter, entitled Physics in Everyday Life.

Thinking and communicating in a logical manner does not come instinctively to most people and, indeed, the scientist's logic may not necessarily always be that of the listener.

There is a story told of a construction firm that started hiring people for the first time since the end of the recession. It was announced that candidates for jobs would be interviewed at 7 a.m. on Monday at a certain location.

An eager young man was the first to apply for a position. The foreman looked at him quizzically and asked him, 'Well, lad, what can you do?'

'I can do anything, sir,' he said.

'Well, let's take this step by step,' said the foreman. 'First, can you make a cup of tea?'

'Yes, I can,' said the young man.

Then there was a long pause. 'Now, can you drive a forklift truck?' asked the foreman.

The young man was clearly nonplussed by this question and said nothing for quite some time. Then he looked up into the face of the foreman and asked, 'Just how big would this teapot be?'

In this illustration, the logic of the foreman was to develop a profile of the applicant and relate that to a job vacancy. The young man, on the other hand, was trying to see how making tea and driving a forklift truck might be related in any logical fashion and could find only one solution to that problem.

Efficient communication between one person and another is always difficult and communication between the scientist and a non-scientist an extreme case of this problem. Communication without jargon, embellishment, or unnecessary detail is an art and a skill that can take a lifetime to acquire. When all is said and done, the ability to answer questions that students and members of the public wish to ask is perhaps just as valuable as teaching people what you think they ought and need to know. Both endeavours are important.

Chapter Twenty

Physics in Everyday Life

A Canadian physicist was touring the west of Ireland by car recently, at peace with the world, and enjoying the vivid beauties of nature. Suddenly he, for it turned out to be a he, saw another car approaching rapidly from the opposite direction. As it passed him, the driver of the other vehicle pulled down the window, looked him straight in the eye, and shouted the one word 'pig'. At this our physicist friend became somewhat nonplussed, but quickly recovering his composure, put his head out of the window in the direction of the receding car, and gave vent to as fine a string of rude epithets as had ever been heard of in the region. In fact, he was only halfway through his diatribe when he hit the pig!

The moral of this apocryphal tale is quite simple: communication between two people is never easy and the ability to communicate effectively is an art to which few aspire and at which fewer still are successful. Communicating science to a non-scientist is a particular instance of this problem.

★

One day, in the summer of 1991, the local CBC AM radio station 990 in Winnipeg decided to launch a weekly six-minute science programme in which real world questions in the realm of physics or physical science would be posed by members of the local community and be answered by a resident scientist, specifically, the author of this book. The question as to whether appropriate questions would be forthcoming found an early answer, but the diversity, the perceptive nature of the questions, and the lack of precise and unambiguous answers, made the whole exercise an exciting and challenging one, for everyone concerned.

In the paragraphs which follow, a selection of real life problems submitted by listeners is offered along with the solutions presented on the programme. It will be clear that all involve aspects of physics unlikely to be addressed explicitly in standard high school or university teaching materials.

The very first question asked by a listener involved the topic of thixotropy. Technically, thixotropy is a structural property that causes certain gels to liquefy and then to solidify again. The breakdown to the liquid state is a function of time and shear rate. In general, solidity returns over time in the absence of shear. For those who are not familiar with the term gel, gel is a colloidal suspension of a solid in a liquid forming a jelly-like material. Jello is clearly a gel. The question asked by the listener was quite simple and is reproduced here in the listener's own words. 'Occasionally, during the night, I get up and go down to the kitchen, open the fridge, and take out a canister of yoghurt. Sometimes I notice that if it is a new carton and a spoonful of the substance is removed cleanly from the centre of the carton, the hollow left behind in the substance will have filled up with liquid by the time I return in the morning for some additional sustenance. Why has this happened and where has the liquid come from?'

In answer to this question, it is clear that thixotropy of some kind is involved. Once a shear force is applied to a substance that is only marginally solid, in this case by a spoon, the yoghurt is enabled to flow like a liquid while the shear force is being applied. This is known from the behaviour of such materials as margarine, which is solid and only flows when it is actually being spread; tomato ketchup, which has some of this property; and many ceiling paints which consist of a gel which flows only when the paint is being applied.

For those not too familiar with the idea of a shear force, a shear force is applied by hedging shears when a garden hedge is trimmed. In respect of the actual question, I initially had some doubts as to the veracity of the observation, not being a midnight yoghurt fiend myself. However, over coffee it became quite clear that most physicists have directly experienced the phenomenon described by the listener and, as I looked into it, I became convinced that the rationale that I was developing was indeed correct. Specifically, the angle of attack of the spoon generated a shear force followed by liquid flow. Once the hollow was filled with liquid and the shear force removed, the liquid solidified again.

*

On another occasion, when asked by an elderly listener why her eyeglasses got coated with oil on the inside when cooking French fries on the stove, I really doubted that the observation was correct. However, various of my colleagues and members of their families attempted to disprove the facts of the question only to find that the observation was indeed a correct one. This being so, it became essential for the respondent to find justification for the phenomenon Now, it is an interesting fact that whenever oil from a pan is turned into aerosol particles which then fly up under thermal currents past the face of the cook, there is little time for minute particles to attach themselves to the glass of the spectacles. On the other hand, if the spectacles are fairly close to the face, particles of oil may occasionally get trapped behind the eyeglasses and find themselves in semi-static or stagnant air, that is between the face and the glass itself. In this case, such small particles of oil may actually move around in random fashion and tend to coagulate into larger droplets, most of which will tend to migrate towards the coldest surface and condense further there. The inside of the spectacles would seem to be the most likely point to collect aggregates of oil droplets and, if this is indeed the explanation, then we do understand the phenomenon which is described by the listener.

*

On one occasion, towards the end of winter, an unusual questioner came to the fore, being in fact an observant ex-Associate Dean of Science from the University of Manitoba (not a physicist) who had retired to a home near Lake Winnipeg where he exercised his acute observational skills throughout the winter while waiting for the ice to melt and his boat to be made available for distant travel up the lake. The observation was as follows: on a cloudy day in late winter, towards the end of March, with apparently hardly any light filtering through the heavy sky, if an observer looks at a fresh snowbank he or she may be overcome by the brightness of the light that is reflected. The question was: 'How can such perfect whiteness be observed from a snowbank when it appears little light from the sun is reaching ground level and everything around is uniformly grey?'

I think this is an interesting question because it can easily be verified that the brightness of such a bank is indeed overwhelming to the observer and yet the observation that the sky and clouds above seem grey to black is also equally easy to confirm. The most relevant fact in relation to this question is that new snow will perfectly reflect white light that is falling upon it, irrespective of the source. When you look at a cloud and you see it as dark grey, or even black, you see regions that are not transmitting direct sunlight. You are not aware of the light that is actually still being transmitted through the cloud and reaching ground level, and of course any light that reaches your snowbank is likely to be reflected almost perfectly by the crystals that are there. It should also be noted that the light coming through the cloud is diffuse and going in a whole variety of directions on transmission. The diffusely transmitted light from the whole cloud surface within the solid angle acceptable by the snowbank is however available to the snowbank and so one must not be fooled because a cloud looks dark or even that the whole sky looks grey, into thinking that little light is reaching the earth's surface. Indeed, the light is more than substantial under these circumstances, and although the listener's question gave the impression that the light reflected from bank was intense, there was no suggestion that snow blindness would be involved, as might well be the case if one stared continuously at a snowbank when the full direct sunlight was falling upon it. Many skiers know that this can indeed be a problem and most people who engage in that sort of activity should wear some form of eye protection in the form of Polaroid sunglasses or filtering material. So, whereas the observation sounds dramatic and the components involved in it conflicting, there seems little doubt that what is observed is merely what a physicist would qualitatively expect.

★

Following several months of the CBC programme involving problems of everyday physics and personal observation, I found that my wife, Christine, was taking a healthy interest in the programme. The main point here was that she had a scientific question that she kept asking her husband from time to time and which had not as yet received an answer and so she determined to call the listener line on CBC to attempt to obtain a response from the scientific correspondent, Jasper McKee. The question itself was simple and the observation was easy to confirm. However, the explanation of the phenomenon was not instantly clear to me and I am afraid I prevaricated to the point at which the desperate measure of calling the CBC was next on her list. The problem was as follows: the number of the McKee house on Wellington Crescent is 1443. The number is displayed in large brass letters and it does not take a very observant person to see that whereas the two middle letters, that is to say the two fours, are bright and shiny, the two numbers on the outside are tarnished, pitted, and rough despite the fact all four were originally erected at the same time. Now there were various models for the phenomenon that came to mind. One was that perhaps rain falling on these letters from the lamp supports above was falling preferentially on the outer two letters rather than the centre ones and eventually, through acidic action, destroying those two. The main problem was that it had not rained in Winnipeg, in any significant way, for about five years and to depend on that explanation would seem to be flying in the face of reality. The second possibility was that the prevailing wind from west to east was blowing dirt from the prairie or from the yard across the surface of the four numbers and preferentially cleaning, as in sandblasting, some numbers more than others. Had that, of course, been the case, the number one would have been most shiny and the others less so, as one moved to the right and from one through the two fours to the three. This is not in accordance with the facts of the question. So, in desperation and being obliged to attempt to answer this question the following Monday, I sat down at lunch with a colleague in mechanical engineering, who has just become an Emeritus Professor, Kris Tangri, and while we were passing the time of day, I told him of my quandary and problem and asked him if he had any idea what the solution to this problem might be. Dr Tangri, without thinking for a moment, said that the numbers clearly come from different batches. He indicated that the two fours must be from a good batch of numbers in which the alloy was of quality but that the one and the three are not really of brass composition at all. They are a mixture of copper and zinc that is not within the proportions of alpha brass or perhaps even beta brass, for that matter. Up to thirty-six per cent in proportion of zinc is found in a quality brass. For proportions larger than that and up to forty-five, you will have a brass that is less ductile but stronger. But beyond this, and also for a much lower proportion of zinc, you will not be dealing with brass but with a mixture of copper and zinc in unusual proportions. Now, once you have separate pockets or small cells of copper and zinc randomly displaced throughout the body of the material, the possibility of chemical action becomes a real one. You can have little galvanic cells dotted throughout the surface which, if joined by some piece of debris or conducting material in the form of dust or something else, may actually, through chemical action, generate a cell that will, through electrical activity, generate holes or pitting in the material. The surface of the numbers one and three is certainly consistent with such a happening and the overall roughness of the surface which was originally smooth may be attributable to electrochemical action. My wife found the solution acceptable and no protest was raised by the listening public.

★

A phenomenon noticed by a number of listeners, and seeming somewhat unlikely to most scientists, was that on stirring certain varieties of tomato soup, once stirring had been completed and the thickish liquid had ceased to rotate, instead of all motion ceasing forthwith, the soup would tend to rotate momentarily in the opposite direction to that of the original stirring. It took some time to confirm that this was indeed the case and it certainly only applies to certain varieties of commercial soups. However, a phenomenon that has been known for a considerable time and is best demonstrated in respect of solutions of polyethylene oxide of high molecular weight, seems to be operative here. It is viscoelasticity, noticeable in many long chain molecules. There is in fact a trend towards the development of designer starches that operate on the basis of such viscoelasticity. When the moving, swirling soup is almost at rest because of friction with the sides of the saucepan, the surface layer continues to move although the lower soup has come to rest. The surface layer is then pulled back by an elastic force between it and the lower soup, and the direction of swirl is thereby reversed for a short while. The surprising fact to many people is that there are liquids which possess such elasticity. However, being liquid they also can be viscous and resist flow. Viscoelasticity is typical of high polymers such as jellies, dough, and even soap solutions. The polyethylene oxide mentioned earlier is particularly useful in demonstrating viscoelasticity, and soup that is swirling behaves in similar fashion. The detailed explanation would be that, after stirring, air bubbles mixed in and trapped in liquid retrace their movements when the stirring is suddenly stopped. This is the elastic property that they possess. The angle through which they recoil is a measure of the elasticity of the liquid. Some varieties of soup, from tomato through Scotch broth, exhibit this phenomenon and it has been identified by certain of our listeners in their culinary activity.

★

Now, strangely enough, the swirling of soup is not the only illustration of viscoelasticity in the kitchen. One evening a woman called me at home in relation to a rather immediate problem that had arisen. After preparing a hot white sauce in the usual way she poured it over a hot dessert allowing it to cool briefly. On inserting a spoon, the sauce then apparently exploded, covering ceiling and wall with sauce fragments. How could this have happened?

The answer lies in the nature of cornstarch. Cornstarch, the essential ingredient of white sauce, is basically a viscoelastic material. In water solution it can be an elastic solid when mixed in a one to one ratio. The solution will withstand hammer blows from above while flowing thickly in the horizontal plane. Indeed, pouring a one-to-one mixture of cornstarch and water down the sink can result in perfect blocking if any further evaporation of the mixture occurs. The relevance of this fact to white sauce is simply that at a ratio of one part cornstarch to six of water, a palatable sauce is generated. At a lower ratio something between a delicious liquid and an elastic solid can be achieved. If a sauce rich in cornstarch is prepared and cooled the elastic solid may compress air below it and on puncturing produce a significant explosion once the pressure is released. This mechanism after all is similar to the generation of seaspray when the crest of a wave falls into a preceding trough. The moral to this story seems to be – go easy on the cornstarch and all will be well.

★

Two further culinary questions require answers. Firstly, why does food cooked in a microwave oven appear to cool more quickly than that in a conventional oven? Secondly, is it true that the presence of salt in food inhibits cooking in a microwave oven? The answer to the first is related to the nature of the food and the cooking time: Cooking occurs as a result of the absorption of microwave energy, and the amount absorbed with depth depends on the frequency of the microwaves. For a frequency (typical) of 2450 MHz only the first two centimetres of meat absorb energy and the rest is gradually heated by conduction. If the piece of meat is small, heat from all directions will flow to the centre with ease. Indeed, heat will be generated in the centre directly, and because heat is lost largely from the surface, the inside of a small piece may be hotter than the outside. A larger piece on the other hand, heated by conduction from the surface may still be quite cool in the centre where microwaves do not penetrate. Heat then is conducted away from the surface, and by the time uniform heating is achieved, the surface temperature may have dropped significantly. Surface temperature on removal from an oven is a poor guide to conditions inside. A conventional oven does a better job in general on roasts of considerable size.

As for the question of salty foods, scientists at Leeds University have recently demonstrated that salt in a product, in particular mashed potato or a TV dinner, will result in surface boiling of the food while the inside remains essentially at room temperature. Common salt, monosodium glutamate and other salts screen the centre of food samples from the microwave radiation. The reason for this phenomenon is not entirely clear but it appears that ions from the salts flow as induced electric currents on the surface of salty foods, screening the centre of the product from the microwave radiation. Whatever the details of the explanation, adding salt after cooking rather than before would seem to be a good idea.

*

Finally, a question from a listener to CBC Regina. 'I make two drinks in identical glasses – one is rye and soda water, the other rum and cola. The volume of each is the same as the other. Each glass has three large ice cubes from the same tray added. Why does the ice in the rye and soda melt twenty minutes before that in the rum and cola?

In response let me inform you that experiments in the CBC studios at Regina confirmed the truth of this observation. The explanation is not immediately forthcoming. Both liquors have the same alcohol content by volume. Both contain sugar, as do cola and soda water. The melting of the ice cubes must be accelerated by heat energy carried from the lower regions of each glass by bubbles of carbon dioxide dissolved in the soft drinks prior to pouring. The solubility of CO_2 in cola is if anything greater than in water, so initially one might expect the reverse situation to that described in the question to appertain.

It is my belief that the viscosity of the cola drink is large enough to inhibit flow of bubbles and heat to the surface. I have suggested that studies of the other mixtures, rye and cola and rum and soda water be carried out, and that additional tests involving completely flat soda water and cola be performed. As a poor physicist I have neither the funds nor the time to initiate the ongoing research necessary to solve this problem. I encourage readers to take up the challenge.

*

Other questions I leave as exercises for would-be physicists. What time is it at the North Pole? Why does a coffee drop in a cup dry in concentric rings? How is it that when a beaker of hot water is poured outdoors on ice in winter on the prairies it freezes more quickly than an equal initial volume of water at room temperature? ('What about the second law of thermodynamics?' you say!) Why does chicken in a freezer bag in the freezer have frost all over its surface on removal whereas chicken in a brown bag does not? Why do shower curtains move inward when the shower is in normal operation? These are questions worrying our colleagues out there in the community at large.

*

To conclude this chapter, let me recall an anecdote concerning a first-class academic who not only was a good physicist but believed that he could solve most problems using his existing knowledge and rational thought. He liked to experience new phenomena, mountain climbing, water skiing, solo flying, and so on. One day he was asked if he would take part in a skydiving demonstration. He was told he would like it, so he agreed with alacrity. Unfortunately, he was arrogant enough to ignore all advanced instructions tips and guidelines with the result that when he jumped from the plane he had a minimum of facts available to him. He instinctively reached for the ripcord, but nothing happened. He then pulled every string and toggle available, but all to no avail. As he fell like a stone he suddenly observed to his relief another person coming up to meet him from ground level. The second person was slowing noticeably and our physicist was reaching his terminal velocity so conversation had to be short and crisp. 'Do you know anything about parachutes?' he shouted.

'No! How are you with gas furnaces?' was the faint reply. The moral to this tale is simply that known facts and rational thought may not always do the job.

The answer to even the most simple question is not always obvious, and the questions asked by non-scientists are often those that no physicist would have entertained. Let the search for truth continue.